GIVER OF LIFE

The Holy Spirit in the Creed and
in the Christian life today

Jane Williams

Published in Great Britain in 2025
SPCK
SPCK Group
Studio 101
The Record Hall
16–16A Baldwin's Gardens
London EC1N 7RJ
www.spckpublishing.co.uk

Text copyright © Jane Williams 2025

This edition copyright © Society for Promoting Christian Knowledge 2025

Jane Williams has asserted her right under the Copyright, Designs and Patents Act, 1988, to be identified as Author of this work.

All rights reserved. No part of this book may be reproduced or transmitted in any form or by any means, electronic or mechanical, including photocopying, recording, or by any information storage and retrieval system, without permission in writing from the publisher.

SPCK does not necessarily endorse the individual views contained in its publications.

The author and publisher have made every effort to ensure that the external website and email addresses included in this book are correct and up to date at the time of going to press. The author and publisher are not responsible for the content, quality or continuing accessibility of the sites.

Unless otherwise noted, Scripture quotations are taken from the New Revised Standard Version of the Bible, Anglicized Edition, copyright © 1989, 1995 by the Division of Christian Education of the National Council of the Churches of Christ in the USA. Used by permission. All rights reserved.

EU GPSR Authorised Representative
LOGOS EUROPE, 9 rue Nicolas Poussin, 17000, La Rochelle, France
Email: Contact@logoseurope.eu

British Library Cataloguing-in-Publication Data
A catalogue record for this book is available from the British Library

ISBN 978–0–281–09122–5
eBook ISBN 978–0–281–09123–2

1 3 5 7 9 10 8 6 4 2

Typeset by Manila Typesetting Company
First printed in Great Britain by Clays Limited

eBook by Manila Typesetting Company

Produced on paper from sustainable sources

I would like to thank the McDonald Agape Foundation, and Peter McDonald in particular, not only for the support offered to me personally but also for enabling St Mellitus College's ambitious and exciting exploration of the Creed through the Nicaea Project, 2023–2027

Jane Williams is the McDonald Professor in Christian Theology at St Mellitus College. Her recent books include *The Sacraments* (2024), *The Art of Christmas* (2021) and *The Art of Advent* (2018).

'Jane Williams is a wise and thoughtful guide to what we profess about God, to who and what we say that God is, since that's what guides our own faith and practice. *Giver of Life* is a master class in Christian belief and in how the creeds shape us day on day.'
Dr Greg Garrett, Carole McDaniel Hanks Professor of Literature and Culture at Baylor University, and author of *The Gospel according to James Baldwin*

'This marvelous book is both a gem and a prism. Refracting the ancient insights of Augustine and the Cappadocians, Williams invites us to give into the shining, life-giving mystery of the Holy Spirit. Our 'creedal' faith is ultimately a commitment to shaping the world in response to the loving action of God.'
Professor James K.A. Smith, Department of Philosophy, Calvin University, and author of *How to Inhabit Time*

'This is a wonderful and remarkably accessible account of how Christians in the earliest centuries of the Church's history, thought and talked about the Holy Spirit. It is especially helpful, as the Holy Spirit can sometimes be given less attention than deserved in discussions of Christian doctrine. This book is perfect for those who want to better understand the Holy Spirit as a person within the Trinity and in the context of the creeds. It provides a rare opportunity to consider what this history means for believers today.'
Dr Selina Stone, Lecturer in Theology and Ethics, School of Divinity, University of Edinburgh, and author of *Tarry Awhile: Wisdom from Black Spirituality for People of Faith*

'This is an extraordinarily rich meditation on what the Nicene Creed says about God, and in particular the Holy Spirit. Jane Williams takes us deep into the luminous mystery of this remarkable text and on every page throws up new insights and

fresh perspectives on what it means to say we believe in the Holy Spirit.'
The Rt Revd Dr Graham Tomlin, Director, Centre for Cultural Witness, Lambeth Palace Library, and author of *Navigating a World of Grace: The Promise of Generous Orthodoxy*

Contents

Introduction	1
1 A creedal world	5
2 The case for the Holy Spirit: the Cappadocian Fathers	16
3 The case for the Holy Spirit: Augustine of Hippo	35
4 The Holy Spirit defended: summarising the arguments	47
5 The Holy Spirit in the Creed	55
6 The Holy Spirit, the Giver of Life	87
Notes	125
Suggested further reading	135

Introduction

In 325, representative leaders of the Christian Church worldwide, newly emerging from persecution and able, for the first time, to meet and discuss legally, agreed upon a 'creed': a statement of faith that was intended to summarise the Bible's witness to God's action in Jesus Christ. Seventeen hundred years later, that creed, with some developments, is still widely used across all Christian denominations, as it will be for the foreseeable future.

This book arises partly out of the opportunity to celebrate 1,700 years of creedal living but also partly out of years of teaching an introductory course on doctrinal and systematic theology shaped by the declarations of the Nicene Creed. What has emerged most strikingly through that teaching is the need for a fuller understanding of what the Creed has to say about the Holy Spirit.

The Creed has shaped Christian worship and theology for 1,700 years and will continue to do so long after 2025. This book is unlikely to have such lasting impact, but I hope that its use will not be confined to 'Nicaea year', instead becoming part of a growing theology of the Holy Spirit, the Giver of Life.

This book is intended both for personal use and for group study, and questions are provided to help the reader to engage with the points being made. The chapters build on one another. Chapter 1 outlines what we do and do not mean when we say 'I believe': what kind of response is the Creed expecting of us, and why? Chapters 2 and 3 focus in on a pivotal time in the development of the doctrine of the Holy Spirit in the fourth and fifth centuries. In particular, these chapters draw on the work

Introduction

of the Cappadocian Fathers and of Augustine to highlight the perennial questions asked about the Spirit. Is the Spirit really God? If so, is the Spirit a slightly less important God than the Father and the Son? That leads to questions of hierarchy in God – are some persons of the Trinity more equal than others? And also to questions about time – does the 'real' God come before the Son and the Spirit? Is the doctrine of the Trinity really what the Bible means by 'God'? And what difference does it make, anyway? Chapter 4 briefly summarises the arguments made by the Cappadocians and Augustine. It then looks directly at what the Creed says about the Holy Spirit, the Giver of Life. The final chapter builds a theology of the Holy Spirit that connects God's reality with our own calling as disciples. 'We believe' that God is like this, Father, Son and Holy Spirit, and that we are called to a life as sisters and brothers of the Son, children of the one Father, through the Holy Spirit. The Creed names our human vocation as it declares its trust in this God.

In this book, I have tried not to use gendered language about God, where it is avoidable, though I do continue to use masculine pronouns for Jesus, the incarnate Son. The language of Father and Son is so deeply embedded in Scripture and tradition, so unique to the Christian understanding of the loving and relating reality of God, that it is not easily replaced. Attempts to use instead descriptions of God's actions, like Creator, Redeemer and Sanctifier, do not quite work for several reasons. One is that the doctrine of the Trinity invites us to see the whole of God – Father, Son and Holy Spirit – involved in the entirety of God's action towards us. No one 'person' acts without the others, despite their distinctive roles in our encounter with God. A second drawback is that, as we shall see, 'Father', 'Son' and 'Holy Spirit' are not God's proper names, like Hilary, Rowan or Pip; they designate the internal relational being of God, in which each 'person' is constituted in relation

Introduction

to the others, rather than by what they do. Finally, Creator, Redeemer, Sanctifier, or other such designations, are entirely about God in relation to us, whereas the Creed summarises the Christian tradition's declaration that in God's very being, eternally and transcendently, God is relational in a way that is echoed by our human words 'Father, Son and Holy Spirit'.

But that does not mean that God is masculine, or more like a man than a woman. God is spirit; God is not a created being, living in time and acted upon by other bodies. When the Son becomes human, he does so as a man, but his humanity is, importantly, representative of the whole human race. If that is not so, then non-male human beings are still to be saved. Jesus Christ unites humanity, not just maleness, with God's saving action.

Unthinking parallels between the maleness of Jesus and the maleness of God have been very damaging and have distracted from the theology of the generous abundance of God's presence and action in all that God has made. The unthinking transference between human and divine fatherhood has made God unapproachable for many whose experience of human fathering has been poor or even abusive. The words we use have consequences; words have a life of their own in the imaginations of those who use them and hear them, and that means that religious language needs to be used with extreme care and sensitivity.

Some have suggested that the Holy Spirit might be able to carry some apparently missing feminine language into the Godhead. The arguments used are slightly specious, based on, for example, the fact that the Hebrew word for 'breath' is a feminine noun, *ruach*. But the French word for a table, *la table*, is also a feminine noun and brings with it no particular feminine resonances. It is also questionable whether designating as feminine the most self-effacing person of the Trinity, who

Introduction

seems to be entirely shaped by relationship to Father and Son language, really empowers the feminine.

As we have become more properly conscious of the damage done by sexism, these issues of how to address God appropriately have grown more pressing. Augustine unselfconsciously says that we are fed from the breasts of the Father; Julian of Norwich calls Jesus our Mother; medieval mystics often see the Christian soul as feminine in relation to God, whatever the gender of the Christian.[1] But all of these usages come from a time of patriarchy, where even imaginative and non-standard language about God did not fundamentally challenge the basic notions of the maleness of God or the subjugation of women.

In speaking of the Holy Spirit, it is important to retain the personal reality of the Spirit, which rules out calling the Holy Spirit 'it'. I have already suggested that 'she' might not be a helpful pronoun for the Spirit, but since the Spirit is the person of the Trinity not named by a masculine relationship, it does seem unnecessary to use masculine pronouns for the Spirit. It might be that they/them pronouns will provide a solution, going forward, as these indicate true personhood with a refusal of simple binaries. The challenge is to distinguish between 'they' as singular and plural pronouns. In the end, I have tried to avoid using gendered pronouns at all in relation to the Holy Spirit, in order to attempt to emphasise that God is not male.

For some readers, this whole discussion of gender will be irrelevant; others will find my approach either much too conservative or much too untraditional. This might give the opportunity for discussion in groups, or for individual readers to note and analyse their reactions.

1
A creedal world

The Holy Spirit is a comparative latecomer to the formal creeds, as we shall see. But the titles attributed to the Spirit in the Nicene Creed are wide-ranging and encourage a deep theology of the Spirit. And in the creedal statements found in worship and Christian initiation that predate the systematic creedal process, the Holy Spirit has always been fundamental. People are baptised in the name of the Father, Son and Holy Spirit, who is One God. St Basil the Great uses this as one of the central arguments for the fact that Christians clearly demonstrate their belief in the full divinity of the Spirit, and – whether consciously or unconsciously – know that the Spirit is the entrance point for faith.

The Holy Spirit brings us into the life that is shaped by Jesus, the life that is the Son's response to the Father, lived out in our world, so that we, too, can be invited into it. This is an assertion that this book will explore through the brief, intriguing statements made about the Holy Spirit in the Christian creeds, particularly the one usually called the Nicene Creed. The creeds themselves, like the Bible, are part of the work of the Holy Spirit in depicting a world in which God is real and active and in which human beings respond – in a whole variety of ways, good and bad, constructive and destructive, but always with the certainty that they are not the only, or even the main, shapers of the world and its history. This is the world as described with admirable brevity by the Creed.

Precisely because the Creed is so succinct, it is easy to miss what it is actually describing and what it is that we are claiming when we affirm that we believe these things. In particular, it is not always clear where the Creed's description of the work of the Holy Spirit comes from, and how many of the final lines of the creeds are affirmations not primarily about the Church and the final future of the world but actually about the work of the Holy Spirit.[1] This ambiguity is telling; as we explore the Creed's declarations about the Holy Spirit, the reason for this blurring will become clearer.

The Bible regularly shows the relationship between human beings and God as one that is freely enabled by God and in which human beings are given the dangerous dignity of choice. Extraordinary as it might seem, human beings can choose not to believe and trust in the One who is the source of their life and without whom they would cease to exist. In the Genesis creation story, there is a tree, 'the tree of the knowledge of good and evil' (Genesis 2:17), which should have remained a myth but is brought into actuality by human choice; at the culmination of the long story of God's liberation and miraculous provision for the freed slaves of Pharaoh, Joshua offers the people a choice again: 'choose this day whom you will serve' (Joshua 24:15); in the presence of the incarnate God, some 'did not accept him' (John 1:11). Ephesians describes a whole spiritual realm that is egging us on to choose our own destruction rather than the reality of God's gift (Ephesians 6:12–17). As Ephesians makes clear, what we choose, over and over again, is – as Joshua writes – whom we will serve. With pithy brevity, Jesus says, 'No one can serve two masters' (Matthew 6:24).

What is at stake here is what we will allow to shape us and our world. Our longings and desires and our responses to them make us the people we are and dictate how we behave towards one another. We might not admit to ourselves that we are choosing our 'god', the one to whom we will offer our service, but that is, in fact, what we are doing. We might persuade ourselves

A creedal world

that we are in control of our choices rather than that they are controlling us. Most of our choices look small and insignificant, and it is easy to miss the way in which they mount up and lead us in a particular direction. The Bible narrative suggests that we are faced, over and over again, with choices, some small and some large but all part of the magnificent freedom given by God to God's creatures. Wilfully, we blind ourselves to God urging us to choose life (Deuteronomy 30:19; John 1:12), preferring smaller gods who offer little, even while requiring everything.

This choice, with everything it entails about how we view the world, is what creeds are all about. Christianity is regularly described as a 'creedal' faith. The word comes from the Latin *credo*, 'I believe', and it suggests a particular kind of personal and communal claiming or declaring of faith. There are two main aspects to this description: first of all, even those brought up in a Christian family or in a culture that believes itself to hold 'Christian values' come to a point in their life of faith when they have to choose whether they are 'Christians', followers of Christ. Whom will they serve? And that leads on to the second aspect of what it is to be a creedal faith: accepting this faith as our own entails a commitment to seeing the world in a particular way, together with others and dependent upon the character and action of God. There is always this double vision in creeds: 'I believe' but also 'we believe'. If this is what I believe about the world, then it is not just my private faith; it encompasses all of reality.

These two aspects of a creedal faith are closely related, but while one is a decision taken – 'I am a Christian, by my own choice' – the other is often a lifetime's work: what does it mean to say that 'I believe' that the world has a particular character because it is the work of a particular God? How does that affect my actions and my understanding, day by day? Of course, people who declare their faith at a particularly decisive moment in an act of commitment might change their minds and decide that they do not, after all, believe in or want to be followers of Christ, but even those who continue to believe will have doubts and different interpretations of how to live a faithful life in different circumstances. Having a faith based in creedal affirmations does not take away human choice and discipleship; quite the contrary, in fact. We say, 'I believe,' or, 'We believe,' not, 'I know,' or, 'We know.' And that in itself is part of the dynamic of what is going on in creeds: the God in whom we say we believe is apparently one who invites response and responsibility, not one who simply declares the answer and requires mindless obedience. Already, in the very act of saying, 'I believe,' we are stating something about the character of God and our response. And that interaction between what God is like and how we respond is part of the active sphere of the Holy Spirit. We affirm something that needs to be lived into; it is not abstract knowledge but a calling into a vocation to be 'daughters and sons' like the Son. This calling and the life that it leads to are gifts of the Holy Spirit.

Both aspects of what we mean by saying that Christianity is a creedal faith have a communal side as well as a personal one. The God whom the creeds describe invites each one to say, 'I believe,' but what we say we believe is that this is the God who created all that is 'seen and unseen'. This is not just our personal God but the God of all reality. Creeds, then, generally start out as a shared declaration, in which, together, we say, 'This is the world I believe in.' A group of people who together say, 'I believe,' also demonstrate something that is fundamental to the character of God, as shown in the creeds: God draws people together, as though there is a level of understanding and action that cannot be accessed by an individual alone; there is something about creedal reality that requires community and, in the Creed, that community of faith flows on from the statements about the

Holy Spirit. The 'one holy catholic and apostolic Church' comes under the wings of the Holy Spirit.

The first aspect of faith, where a distinct decision is made by an individual, might well happen alone, or it might happen under the impact of something immensely personal, which makes us see ourselves and our world differently. The old evangelical description of this as 'asking the Lord Jesus into your heart' is one way of describing this moment of choice, though there are many other descriptions. Some can name the moment of clarity, whereas for others the process is almost unnoticeable. But this choice, however it arrives, brings with it a whole community of faith that is – like it or not – now part of the world that we have committed to in saying, 'I believe.'

Except in very unusual circumstances, such as in persecution, where faith cannot be publicly declared, the personal decision must also be made in front of those others who have chosen to say, 'We believe.' In most traditions, wherever possible, that happens in the context of baptism or confirmation. The sacramental incorporation of the individual into the community is also the work of the Holy Spirit: it is the Holy Spirit who makes ordinary water into the water of new life in Christ.[2]

This point of public declaration is the first setting for creedal statements like the one found in the Church of England rite of baptism. The new member declares that they believe and trust in one God, Father, Son and Holy Spirit, and that this will involve a change of life from one lived as though good and evil are equal and opposite choices, or where choices are value-neutral, to one lived in the faith that there is only one source of all things: the goodness of God, which shapes all the rest of our choices. And when the person to be baptised has affirmed that faith, the gathering of Christians responds, 'This is our faith.' Personal and communal necessarily echo one another because we do not live in private worlds but in a shared one.

A creed is, then, first of all an act of faith: we believe the world to be like this, and we believe it on the grounds of how God is to be found and trusted. We believe it for ourselves, and our faith is strengthened and upheld by the faith of the community. Believing this rules out other ways of seeing the world because there is only one God, the source and the goal of all that is, and that God has decisively been made known through Jesus Christ. This is a world-defining faith, which cannot easily be set alongside other possible alternative views of the world. Either this is true, or it is not.

In the face of such a large claim, creeds developed a further function, which was to clarify more precisely what 'we believe'. A creedal faith that rules out picking and choosing among various divine beings or ways of living needs to be very careful about what it claims and what it is asking of those who say, 'We believe.' The process that led, eventually, to the evolution of a largely standardised set of creeds over the first four to five Christian centuries was a gruelling and often bad-tempered one partly because it mattered so much.[3]

It is hard to take a high view of the guidance of the Holy Spirit through this creedal process, given the politicking and backstabbing that frequently accompanied each phase of the journey and the way in which disagreement over several contested clauses of the creeds split Christians apart. The same could be said about the whole history of the people of God; even the Bible is a source of profound disagreement among Christians of different traditions: how to use it, how to interpret it, how to apply it. And yet it will be the argument of this book that this does not mean that the Holy Spirit is not present and active. Instead, it tells us something of the kind of process that we are involved in when we encounter this God and are brought into encounter with one another. This God, maker of all things, enters into the reality of history in Jesus Christ. And, in the ongoing work of the Holy Spirit, breathing the Christ-shaped calling through all that is, this God continues to create a reality that is genuinely free and different from God and yet able to carry God's presence and reality. God does not overrule created beings; God made them and loves them as creatures, not as failed gods. The creed tells us that real history is capable of bearing the full presence of God in Christ. The creed is talking about actual events, full of actual people, as well as reminding us that this never becomes just our world, empty of God.

Creeds, then, affirm a chosen way of living, which sees the world as beginning and ending with the action of God, inviting us to live in this reality. This is not an arbitrary choice but one based in the paradigm-shifting event of the coming of Jesus Christ into history. Both the content of the creeds and the process we enter into as we commit to them offer insights into what we mean when we say, 'We believe.'

The Nicene Creed

Saying I/we believe is part of the character of Christianity, and creedal statements go back to our earliest records: the New Testament has several. 'Jesus is Lord' is probably the simplest (cf. 1 Corinthians 12:3), though it also reminds Paul's hearers that what they are tempted to think of as their choice is only made possible by the Holy Spirit. Much more complex is 1 Timothy 3:16:

Without any doubt, the mystery of our religion is great:

He [Jesus] was revealed in flesh,
vindicated in spirit,
seen by angels,
proclaimed among Gentiles,
believed in throughout the world,
taken up in glory.

The Philippians 2 statement about the incarnate Christ's self-emptying is generally thought to be quoting something that would be familiar to its hearers, something already in circulation before the letter was written and so part of how the earliest Christians understood their faith in Christ. Developing liturgy and hymnody played their part in establishing short and memorable summaries of faith.

That makes it unsurprising that it was to creedal formulae that the Church of the first few Christian centuries turned when disagreements about the fundamentals of the faith became rife. The process that produced the Nicene Creed was not invented for the new purpose that controversy opened up, though it required a new level of theological argument and sophistication and a change of direction. This Creed had a negative as well as a positive purpose, to rule out as well as to affirm.

A number of currents converged in the fourth century to result in a creed which largely focuses on the relationship between God, the eternal Father, and Christ, the only Son, who becomes a human being, Jesus.[4] The emperor, Constantine, declared himself a follower of the Christian God, giving Christians safety from persecution and space to explore the faith and offer it on a larger stage. Constantine required Christian leaders to put on a show of unity and to step confidently into public life to give greater weight to his decision to put his eggs into the Christian basket.

At the same time, varied readings of the Bible, Jewish theology and the religious/philosophical world of the day were producing very different accounts of the relationship of God to Christ. Things came to a head around the teaching usually ascribed to a learned preacher, Arius, who was making a strong and persuasive theological case that the Son is not eternally part of the nature of God. Many people thought that Arius was probably right: his description allowed a continuation of

Jewish monotheism, without qualification; it chimed well with the philosophical description of the divine as untouched by the physical and material world; and it was able to draw on several biblical passages that seemed to say something similar.

But, as Arius's opponents pointed out, what Arius was also offering was a description of the world that was largely left untouched by the incarnation. According to Arius, 'God' did not really become 'human' and was not to be encountered in the person of Jesus Christ. The life, death, resurrection and ascension of Christ were primarily illustrative rather than fundamental to what we believe about the nature of God and our relationship with God, the world and each other. Is a God who will not, cannot or simply does not become incarnate the same as a God who does? Is a world in which God will not, cannot or simply does not become incarnate the same as one in which God comes to live with us? In retrospect, the answer seems obvious, but it took some time for that to become clear.

Under those circumstances, it is not surprising that the densest and longest section of the Creed is devoted to an explicit and unambiguous statement of the relationship between Father and Son: there is no God who is not this God, always. There is no world that is not the creation of this God, who makes it and comes to live in it, in real history. This God is One but is not undifferentiated. God is Father, Son and Holy Spirit always, not just in history, not just as we come to encounter God but in God's very being.

The earliest version of the Nicene Creed seems to have stated belief in the Holy Spirit but without further elaboration, simply: 'I/we believe . . . and in the Holy Spirit.' There is no suggestion that people did not believe in the Holy Spirit, only that the Spirit's role and divine status was not under the same intense pressure of controversy as that of the Son.[5]

What followed the first Council of Nicaea and the creedal statement it produced was over a century of continuing 'discussion', and sometimes outright fighting, over what the Creed actually meant to say about the relationship between divine and human being and action in Jesus Christ, the Son. After all, the theological implications were huge and unprecedented – then, as now. It is still impossible to imagine how Jesus can be both fully God and fully human, which is what we say that 'we believe'. Inevitably, power politics also played its part, as definitions put forward by one church leader would be rejected by others as a covert claim to authority, not just a doctrinal statement. The creedal statements divide as well as unite, which seems a bitter irony from a process that describes the world and all its communities as drawing their existence from the One God.

In this process, further statements were added about the divinity and character of the Holy Spirit beyond the simple 'we believe in the Holy Spirit' of the first creed of 325 at Nicaea. There is some evidence of opposition to the elucidation of the role of the Holy Spirit: Basil the Great scornfully shreds the arguments put forward by those who thought that it was not necessary to claim divine personhood for the Holy Spirit, as we shall see.[6] But it is hard to tell how widespread or organised this opposition was. It seems to have come from people who largely agreed on what was being said about the divinity of the Son but thought that it was going too far to describe the Holy Spirit as God, too. At the most, they seem to have argued that the Holy Spirit is inferior to the Father and the Son and only has enough power to do what is required of the Spirit.[7] Basil's brother, Gregory of Nyssa, laughs this out of court with, among other arguments, an analogy: a fire cannot be a bit fiery – it is either a fire or it is not; the same with God: the Holy Spirit cannot be a bit God – the Spirit is either God or not.

In fact, however, the set of affirmations made in the Creed about the Holy Spirit seem to have caused far less controversy than those about the Son, though the full implications of what 'we believe' about the Holy Spirit are far-reaching and vital to the whole creedal process.

Augustine of Hippo and the Cappadocian Fathers give some time to refuting the misunderstandings of the Holy Spirit that were current in their time, many of which continue to come up regularly to this day. It is to their work of constructing a robust theology of the Holy Spirit in the Trinity that we turn next.

Questions for further thought

1 How familiar are you with the Nicene Creed? Is it part of the worship you regularly attend?
2 The Creed says, 'We believe,' not, 'We know.' Do you find that a liberating or a frightening idea?
3 The Creed commits us to the Christian community, not just to personal faith. How do you experience this community?
4 Is a world in which God will not, cannot or simply does not become incarnate the same as one in which God comes to live with us? How might you want to respond?

2

The case for the Holy Spirit: the Cappadocian Fathers

The process that led to the realisation that the God in whom we believe is One God – whose Oneness is in the shared reality of Father, Son and Holy Spirit – was a complex one because the idea is complex. Our brains and imaginations simply cannot compute this idea, and we instinctively describe God either in terms that undermine the divine unity, concentrating on Threeness, or in terms that undermine the divine Trinity, concentrating on unity. Yet what the Creed says is that to declare belief in One God, who is Father, Son and Holy Spirit, is not an optional extra for Christians: we cannot claim our theological description of the world and our place in it unless God is like this.

The description of God as Father, Son and Holy Spirit was not dreamed up by people who liked complicated ideas and had nothing better to do with themselves; it was hammered out under the pressure of the incarnation: what must be true about God if Jesus reveals God's nature and offers God's mercy and salvation? What does that say about Jesus? What does that say about revelation? All the usual methods and sources for theological conversation came into play: how do we interpret what the Bible has to say on this? What does the Christian practice of the Church suggest that we believe? How can we make sense of this in terms of the concepts and language available to us? Does this all enable us to engage better as disciples?[1]

The Creed, and the process which led to its compilation, takes for granted that we are not encountering a new god in Jesus but God as known by the Hebrew people and as revealed in the Hebrew Scriptures. This is the God who made everything, freely, under no constraints and without any help from other divine beings. This is the God who chose to make human beings 'in God's image' and gave them freedom to act in creation. God as encountered in the Old Testament is deeply, faithfully relational, calling human beings to know God and to show God to others. God does not remain at a distance, unable or unwilling to communicate except through secondary means, whose messages must always be compromised by being second hand. Although God often speaks and acts through prophets, judges and kings, there is always a careful distinction between God and God's messengers: the prophet declares 'the word of the Lord' given to them to pass on, while remaining clearly a human messenger, not a demi-god. Kings rule under God's authority, and their reigns end if they are unfaithful and lead people astray from their deepest allegiance, which is to God, not to the king.

There is, then, some obvious continuity of character, the creedal process argues, between God as depicted in the Old Testament and God as revealed in Jesus Christ. But strikingly, in Jesus, God's interaction with the world is even more directly attributable to God than the 'word of the Lord' that the prophets give. In Jesus, God comes to live directly, as the Son, in what God has made. Jesus does not fulfil the role of a prophet, declaring a particular message at a particular moment but otherwise being an ordinary, fallible human being. Instead, everything Jesus does, says and is is revelatory of God. Jesus is the message.

A similar process of reasoning goes on in relation to the practices of the Christian Church. Baptism and Eucharist are not just memorials to a great dead prophet but a participation in the new human life made possible by Jesus' life, death, resurrection and ascension. God can and will enter into created reality.

The creeds show the reasoning that went into making sense of this experience of the presence and action of God in our human world, our human history, in Jesus Christ the Son. As we shall see, concepts and language were stretched to their limit and often radically repurposed to fit their new tasks. Ideas were taken from Judaism and philosophy, both of which found the Christian claims about the incarnation unfathomable. The Nicene Creed says that Jesus the Son is 'true God from true God, begotten not made; one in being with the Father; through him all things were made', trying to rule out some of the other options. Whatever we mean by 'God' is what we are talking about when we talk about the Son; and this is what 'for us and for our salvation, came down from heaven and was incarnate'.

The road to this conclusion was not straightforward and has to be re-argued continually. But in general, it was accepted and still stands as a unifying statement of Christian faith.[2] The evolution of the creedal statements about the Holy Spirit was far less tangled, but, precisely for that reason, it is often skated over. The enormity and novelty of what was being said about the incarnate Son required such a profound theological upheaval because both Judaism and the classical philosophical world saw the divine being and reality as transcendent, even if Judaism also knew that God was passionately committed to God's people and world.

But the Holy Spirit does not so obviously defy 'normal' divine categories: the Holy Spirit does not become human. As we shall see, some argued that even if it was conceded that God is Father and Son there was no need to add a third term. 'Spirit' is just another word for 'God' in the Hebrew Scriptures, not at all implying a distinction in God's being. The danger of polytheism still hovered on the edges of Christianity; it was hard enough to maintain the Oneness of God when God was described as Father and Son. Surely adding a third, the Holy Spirit, was simply going too far?

The responses to these doubts about the necessary divinity of the Holy Spirit concentrate on two different but closely related kinds of argument, both based in trying to read the Bible faithfully.

First of all, defenders of the Holy Spirit point to Christian practice, particularly of baptism. Christians are baptised in the threefold name of God, Father, Son and Holy Spirit. This is our entrance into the new life of Christ. Just as the descent of the Holy Spirit on Jesus at his baptism marks the depth of Jesus' identification with us in our humanity, so the descent of the Holy Spirit on us in baptism enables our identification with Jesus in his saving work for us.

The second line of defence draws on what had already been achieved in arguments about the Second Person of the Trinity, the Son, who becomes incarnate in Jesus. We can only receive salvation, forgiveness and participation in the life of God through Christ if Christ is actually God. In Jesus Christ, we are not offered messages about God but God's very self. So also with the Holy Spirit. We receive new life and are enabled to name God as our Father because the Holy Spirit gives us the life made present and invitational in Christ.

These two arguments are closely related because they affirm that the Holy Spirit is the foundation of our continuing entry into the work of God in Christ. Although Jesus has 'ascended' to the Father, and his human historical body is no longer available to his followers, his life-giving presence is not just a past historical event but an ongoing reality through the Holy Spirit. The Holy Spirit is the ongoing access point to the life of God in Christ.

Tighter definitions and more technical language develop to speak about this mysterious and glorious threefold life of the

One God, but what they affirm is simply this: God enables our continuing and saving relationship with the life of God. Foremost among the theologians of the fourth century who lay the foundations for a deeper insight into the doctrine of the Trinity, and so of the reality of the Holy Spirit, are the Cappadocian Fathers and Augustine of Hippo.

The Cappadocian Fathers

Basil the Great, his brother Gregory of Nyssa and their friend Gregory of Nazianzus are hugely significant figures in the history of Christianity for all kinds of reasons. They were strong defenders of the Nicene Creed's description of the Son as 'of one being' with the Father, and also of the full divinity of the Spirit. They also demonstrate why this is not just abstract knowledge but a commitment to shaping the world in response to the loving action of God, Father, Son and Holy Spirit.[3]

Basil and Gregory of Nyssa came from a devout Christian family, some members of which had suffered persecution and sequestration of their property before the conversion of the Emperor Constantine. Basil and his sister, Macrina, explored the monastic life; Basil visited some of the monks and hermits in the Egyptian desert and set out a rule of life, which influenced later monastic foundations. But if his heart lay with this way of life, his sense of duty called him to serve the wider Church, and he became Bishop of Caesarea. Basil established a large social hub where the poor could be fed, the sick cared for and young people educated, coaxing and bullying money from Christians and non-Christians alike to support the work, which he saw as a logical outcome of the theology he defended. If God loves the world and makes human beings in God's image, then Christians must strive to see and nurture that image in others, too.

The Cappadocian Fathers

Gregory of Nyssa, similarly, wrote philosophically sophisticated treatises on, for example, the infinitude of God and the impossibility for human beings of direct knowledge of God. That does not mean our theology is 'wrong', just that it is always going to fall short of the fullness of the divine life because we are created beings with all the limitations of thought and language that entails. For Gregory, theological speculation always leads to prayer, through which we ascend, little by little, to a state of contemplation of the divine, which is not 'knowledge' but is, in some sense, union. Alongside and flowing from his theology, Gregory, like Basil, served as a bishop and tried to use his influence to reconcile warring factions within the Church; his success in this was limited, but he deserves credit for the attempt. Gregory also argued against slavery – one of the first people to do so. He argued that human beings are in the likeness of God, which means that they cannot belong to someone else; furthermore, God acts to set people free from slavery and sin, so who are we to enslave those whom God has freed?[4]

Gregory of Nazianzus was a college friend of Basil's and, like Basil, his heart was drawn to the monastic or solitary life. But between them, his father and Basil persuaded Gregory to enter into active ministry, and he was even, briefly, bishop of the great see of Constantinople at a very fractious time in its history. He clearly did not enjoy the episcopal life and was happy to retreat to Nazianzus again and to live more peacefully. Gregory was a gifted writer and speaker, producing a number of theological orations which, like Gregory of Nyssa's work, make deep connections between theology and the life of prayer and praise.[5]

This biographical detail is important in wrestling with the complex language and ideas that the Cappadocians contribute to an understanding of the Holy Spirit: their theology is based in their lives of prayer, praise and service. They believe that honouring the Holy Spirit is a vital part of the Christian faith.

The arguments

1 Exegeting the Bible

The doctrine of the Trinity developed as a way of trying to be faithful to what the Bible says. If Jesus is the Son of the Father, the 'image of the invisible God' (Colossians 1:15) and the means of our salvation, and if our ongoing access to that saving relationship with God is only through the Holy Spirit, what must that mean for our understanding of God?

Various solutions were offered, most of which did not require the full-blown reimagining of the nature of God as both One and yet also Three. The Cappadocians are particularly insistent, though, that such solutions largely rely on 'proof-texting', making a case from selected verses in the Bible rather than trying to make sense of the whole way in which God interacts with created beings.

Throughout this wrestling with language to find the best way to account for God's actions to us and for us, it is Christology that drives the process. The coming of the Son into human life and history – the incarnation – is a shockingly radical claim, which is either false or else requires a seismic shift in the understanding of the Oneness of God. The incarnation does not claim to reveal a new God but the reality of the One God who has, from creation through to fulfilment, drawn human beings into God's action and life. Christian defences of the doctrine of the Trinity continue to uphold the Oneness of God: this God is the source of all that is; this is the God of the first commandment, 'You shall have no other gods before me' (Exodus 20:3); and of God's mysterious self-naming to Moses, 'I AM WHO I AM' (3:14). The way in which God calls, invites, commands and commits to faithful engagement with people, once seen through the lens of the incarnation, points to God's own being as 'transcendent' in an unusual sense. God is not 'part' of creation and history, but nor is

God loftily unavailable to the world; there is in God an outgoing love that makes sense of all God's interactions with the world, and which Christians, with the author of John's Gospel, name as the possibility of the whole of creation: 'In the beginning was the Word,' John says, 'and the Word was with God and the Word was God' (John 1:1). In other words, God's Oneness somehow has some differentiations in it, and these differentiations are not just present in the way in which God acts in creation but are part of God's own being. God's transcendence is a wholly free, self-giving love, already shared by Father, Son and Holy Spirit in all eternity. God's transcendence is, almost paradoxically, best understood as loving.

Over the first three Christian centuries, this gradually came to be the (largely) accepted reading of the Bible, the only one that could make sense of what we know about God, and how we come to know it, because of the incarnation. But even those who accepted the full divinity of the Son sometimes balked at including the Holy Spirit as the Third Person of the Trinity. The incarnation, the biblical witness to the full presence of God in the human person Jesus, clearly required a doctrinal reaction. But the Hebrew Scriptures already spoke of the Spirit of God as just another word for 'God', and even if the New Testament does seem to develop the Spirit beyond just a synonym, some argued that the Spirit seems to be secondary to and inferior to the two central 'characters' in the being of God: Father and Son. The very vividness of the language of 'Father' and 'Son', which leads us to imagine that we might be able to understand this relationship within God, makes the Holy Spirit even more shadowy. We cannot draw obvious analogies to 'Holy Spirit' from our own experience of relationships.

The Cappadocians are able to use some of the arguments that were used in establishing the divinity of the Son – for example, that something cannot be a little bit God: the Holy Spirit either is God or is not, unless opponents want to argue that there are, in fact, several gods of varying degrees of power and perfection.[6]

But they also draw out some of the implications for what is said in the New Testament about how we come to know God. The incarnation shows us what the Father is like: 'No one has ever seen God. It is God the only Son, who is close to the Father's heart, who has made him known' (John 1:18). But for this revelation of God to become more than interesting information – and more than a revelation through Jesus in history but now ascended into heaven and so no longer directly available to us – God must somehow continue to give us this knowledge and presence constantly. As the Son shows us the Father and invites us to know and love what he shows, so the Spirit shows us the Son and invites us to share the Son's relationship with the Father.

The Cappadocians highlight this noetic circle – this Trinitarian pattern of invitation to knowledge of God. Basil writes, 'Thus the way of the knowledge of God lies from One Spirit through the One Son to the One Father.'[7] They also argue that the Bible enables us to see that this has always been the case. Basil highlights the Spirit's action in the Old Testament: the invitation to the patriarchs, the helping hand offered through the Law, the echoing and re-echoing patterns of divine action through Scripture, the courage in war and the extraordinary signs and wonders witnessed to in Hebrew Scripture as all part of the Spirit's gift of knowledge and participation in the Son to draw us into the life of God.[8]

All three Cappadocians highlight the scriptural witness to the action of the Holy Spirit in the life of Christ. Gregory of Nazianzus builds his case like this:

Christ is born; the Spirit is His Forerunner. He is baptised; the Spirit bears witness. He is tempted; the Spirit leads Him up. He works miracles; the Spirit accompanies them. He ascends; the Spirit takes His place.[9]

Throughout Jesus' earthly ministry, from conception through to resurrection and ascension, the Son and the Spirit are acting in union to draw us to the Father.

This is a strong refutation of those who say that there is no scriptural warrant for speaking of the Holy Spirit as an essential part of the saving work of God in Christ. On the contrary, they argue, it is the Holy Spirit who gives created beings entry into that saving work. To begin with, they point to Jesus' command to us to baptise in the name of the Father, the Son and the Holy Spirit. Baptism is, as Gregory of Nyssa says, fundamental to faith: 'In Holy Baptism, what is it that we secure thereby? Is it not a participation in a life no longer subject to death?'[10] That life is not inherent in creation. It does not come from the water of baptism; it is life that can only be given by God.

The life of faith starts with the Holy Spirit and is enabled by the Holy Spirit throughout. The Cappadocians remind us that 'no one can say "Jesus is Lord" except by the Holy Spirit' (1 Corinthians 12:3). The two faces of 'creedal' faith – the personal commitment and the entry, through baptism, into the shared life of Christ – are both gifts of the Spirit.

Similarly, our growing in faith, both personally and as a community, is part of the life given by the Spirit. The Holy Spirit gives what the name suggests: holiness in the spiritual life. Basil describes this as the Spirit's tender accompanying of those on a journey of faith:

> Through His aid hearts are lifted up, the weak are held by the hand, and they who are advancing are brought to perfection. Shining upon those that are cleansed from every spot, He makes them spiritual by fellowship with Himself.

Giver of Life

> Just as when a sunbeam falls on bright and transparent bodies, they themselves become brilliant too, and shed forth a fresh brightness from themselves, so souls wherein the Spirit dwells, illuminated by the Spirit, themselves become spiritual, and send forth their grace to others.[11]

Notice again the gift-giving economy of life in the Spirit: we are given 'fellowship' with the Spirit both for our own good and so that we can pass it on to others.

Although the Cappadocians would perhaps not have highlighted this aspect of their theology as particularly noteworthy in their culture, to ours, the constant linking of personal and communal in the life of faith given by the Spirit is striking. We have become accustomed to thinking of faith as a personal, intimate relationship between an individual and God, and the Cappadocians would certainly not deny that. But for them, as for the Creed, if that faith is in the One God, source and goal of all things, then it always commits us to others who share this trust and who pray and work for the coming of God's reign. As, with the help of the Spirit, we say, 'Jesus is Lord,' so, with the help of the Spirit, our own gifts are drawn out as gifts to the whole Christian community. The Spirit raises up apostles, pastors, prophets and teachers for the common good, as well as giving the 'charismatic' gifts of healing and tongues (Ephesians 4:11; 1 Corinthians 12:4 ff.).[12] Like the writers of the Epistles, the Cappadocians do not see these as first of all the attributes of a gifted individual subsequently generously shared but as, from start to finish, the work of the Holy Spirit to build a community of witness to and participation in the love of God, Father, Son and Holy Spirit. In the life of the Holy Spirit, that is the definition of a gift: it is given, not owned, and it is for sharing.

Our most basic and essential response to God – prayer and worship – is itself a gift of the Holy Spirit. Gregory of Nazianzus writes:

It is the Spirit in Whom we worship, and in Whom we pray. For Scripture says, God is a Spirit, and they that worship Him must worship Him in Spirit and in truth. And again – We know not what we should pray for as we ought; but the Spirit Itself makes intercession for us with groanings which cannot be uttered; and I will pray with the Spirit and I will pray with the understanding also – that is, in the mind and in the Spirit.[13]

The case for the Holy Spirit, then, is entirely scriptural. The Cappadocians draw attention to the assumptions made throughout the Bible that the action of God towards us is Trinitarian in shape. They particularly emphasise that our own encounter with God's work of creation and re-creation is through the Holy Spirit. The Holy Spirit enables knowledge of and participation in the Son-shaped response of creation to its Creator. Without the presence and action of the Holy Spirit, knowledge of God remains abstract and historical, and does not require or enable response or participation in the life of Christian discipleship.

2 Trinitarian language: numbers and origins

Those who opposed the idea of the Holy Spirit as 'fully God' got confused about how the Oneness of God can be maintained alongside affirmations of the divinity of Son and Spirit. They also pointed to some scriptural passages that seem to suggest a hierarchy, with 'God' at the top sending down commands to the lesser beings, Son and Spirit, and to passages that could be read as saying that first of all there is God alone, and then the Son and the Spirit are 'made' by God. Both of these confusions are inherent in the language we have to use, but the Cappadocians help to expose why they make no sense and help to bring a degree of technical clarity to the naming of the persons of the Trinity and their interconnectedness.

Their starting point is to remind us that we are not in a position to 'describe' God: why would we expect our created, time-bound minds to be able to encompass the uncreated and eternal God? The paradox of what we are saying – God is Three and yet also One – should alert us to the fact that we are saying something essential but also beyond our comprehension. We simply cannot imagine what we are talking about. But equally, that does not mean that what we are saying is untrue. With typical clarity, C. S. Lewis suggests that the relationship between our language about God and the reality of God is like that between a map and the terrain that it shows: the map cannot give you the experience of the desert or the ocean, but it is still a truthful and essential depiction.[14]

In their arguments with opponents, the Cappadocians help to underline appropriate and inappropriate theological confidence. It is appropriate to trust God's self-gift and the Spirit's witness in the Bible and in our life together: 'we believe' this and live accordingly. But it is inappropriate to the point of arrogance to assume that theological language is able to give a full description of God.

For example, one of the areas in which opposition to the understanding of God as Trinity focused was in relation to the 'coming into being' of God, Father, Son and Holy Spirit. Already, that statement has indicated part of the problem in that it is couched in language that assumes sequential movement and a 'before and after'.

The Creed describes the Son as 'begotten' from the Father 'before all ages'. This is deliberately scriptural: John 1:14 tells how the Word that was in the beginning becomes flesh, so that the 'glory' of the Father's Son is visible to us, and John 3:16 makes it clear that this is for our salvation: 'God so loved the world that he gave his only begotten Son' (John 3:16 NKJV).

In the context of John's Gospel, it is clear that 'wherever' and 'whenever' God is, the Word is 'with' God. This is what God in

God's own life eternally is. But the language of 'begetting', in its ordinary context, seems to imply that once there was God the Father, and then the Son came into being. The Cappadocians help to point out the absurdity of the language of before and after when applied to God. God creates time but is not time-bound. To say that there is a before and after in God is to say that God is not infinite and eternal – that, in fact, God is not God. It is also to say that until the Son is 'begotten' the Father is not the Father. Something fundamental in the nature of God would have to change for God, who was not eternally Father, to become Father in 'begetting' the Son.

Instead, the Cappadocians argue that, though we have no choice about using language that implies sequence, we need to be aware that this is a failing of our language, which cannot impose itself on the reality of God. This is how Gregory of Nazianzus explains the reality of God's being, Father, Son and Holy Spirit:

> When did these [Son and Spirit] come into being? They are above all When. But, if I am to speak with something more of boldness – when the Father did. And when did the Father come into being? There never was a time when He was not. And the same thing is true of the Son and the Holy Ghost. Ask me again, and again I will answer you, When was the Son begotten? When the Father was not begotten. And when did the Holy Ghost proceed? When the Son was, not proceeding but, begotten – beyond the sphere of time, and above the grasp of reason.[15]

When we say 'God', then, this is what we mean: God, Father, Son and Holy Spirit. There is never a God who is not constituted like this. But equally importantly, the names we use for God, Father, Son and Holy Spirit are not optional and interchangeable. God is not an undifferentiated whole to which we arbitrarily, on the basis of our encounter with God in different ways, ascribe names. As the quotation we have just used from Gregory makes clear, the Son is said to be 'begotten', and the Spirit is said to 'proceed' eternally and simultaneously.

The description of the Holy Spirit as 'proceeding' rather than 'begotten' is also scriptural. In John 15:26, Jesus promises the Father's gift of the Spirit of Truth, the One who 'proceeds from' or 'comes from' the Father to us at Jesus' behest. The Cappadocians argued that the 'begetting' of the Son is most importantly saying that whatever the Father is, the Son is. There is an identity of divinity between them: the Father does not bring the Son into existence out of some other 'stuff', but the two are both fully divine. But that seems to leave the Holy Spirit in an uncertain position. We know, or think we know, what the analogy of birth is and is not doing in describing the relation between the Father and the Son, but then why is the same language not used about the Holy Spirit, if the Holy Spirit is also as fully God as the Father and the Son are?

Again, the Cappadocians point out that we are importing into God notions that go with our imperfect language. They have already made the case for the full divinity of the Holy Spirit as the one who gives and restores life, who makes the Son visible in and through the incarnation, who works with the Son in redemption and sanctification and so on. But the reading of the Bible, enabled and required by the understanding of God as Trinity, makes it clear that the Son and Spirit are distinguished from each other and from the Father while never separated in being and action. The Spirit's relationship to the Father is not the same as that of the Son, and that difference is expressed in the imperfect but significant language of 'origin'. The Son is 'begotten', and the Spirit 'proceeds'. As always, our language implies a sequence of events with a before and after, but – as with the language of the eternal 'begetting' of the Son and so with the procession of the Spirit – in God's very being, without time or change, God is the Father, Son and Holy Spirit.

Within the life of God there is neither hierarchy nor division, the Cappadocians insist. There is nothing lacking in the Holy Spirit that prevents the Spirit from being the Son; each 'person' within the Trinity is known only in and through the others. Their unity and individuality are both given and received in mutuality. To say 'God the Father' is not to say 'who' God is in a way that then makes the Son and the Spirit only 'god' in a secondary or derivative way. Neither is being 'Father' something that God does, which might suggest a before and after. 'Father', 'Son' and 'Holy Spirit' are best thought of as names that delineate relationship.[16] Although God may be named in many ways, these names are proper to God's own being in a way that, for example, descriptions of God as a rock or as a fortress are not.

This is a profoundly important move on the part of the Cappadocians. When God tells Moses the divine Name (Exodus 3:14), though the Name is utterly mysterious, it is also a signal of God's self-giving. God gives Moses rights; Moses can literally 'name-drop' his relationship with God as the source of his authority. The giving of the Name implies that God is making a commitment to Moses, and, in that sense, making Godself vulnerable to what Moses will do with that knowledge.[17] God is freely and generously initiating a relationship with Moses and the people to whom Moses will announce God's Name. The naming of God is always a relational initiative on God's part.

That background is key to Gregory's point in relation to the names Father, Son and Holy Spirit. We are offered a profound insight into God's own being and God's commitment to us through the freedom to name God. But, as with the great Name of God given to Moses, and with the names Father, Son and Holy

Spirit, what we are invited into remains holy and transcendent. To name God is still to be in the realm of mystery and gift. This is God's invitation to name God in words, not our own cleverness. And there is no way of naming God with the names God offers without also entering into the relationship that God offers. The naming of God is not abstract for human beings but draws them into the relational dynamic that the names themselves imply: Father, Son and Holy Spirit. Perhaps that is one of the necessary correctives of the name 'Holy Spirit': if we are in danger of thinking that we know what the relationship of the Father and the Son is, the Holy Spirit reminds us that we do not and cannot fully comprehend what the eternal relations in God actually are: there is not a simple human analogy to this divine unity and distinction.

The recognition that Father, Son and Holy Spirit are names given in relation to one another, and that they speak always of relating, is one of the greatest breakthroughs in the theology of the Trinity. It helped to combat the assumptions that such language must mean a hierarchy and a before and after in God. It also ruled out the thinking that assumed that one 'bit' of God, the Father, is more fundamentally 'God' than the Son and the Spirit.

But it also brought with it the danger that human imaginations then foregrounded the Threeness of God over the divine unity. In that sense, the word 'relation' is misleading though also illuminating. The Cappadocians deal with this as carefully and as logically as possible. They argue that to number something does not change what it inherently is.[18] Since Father, Son and Holy Spirit are all identically 'God', their order and their threefold names do not change that. They remain the One God, but that One God is always Father, Son and Holy Spirit. We will see that this is something Augustine tries to address in a different way. The emphasis on the unity of God must never undermine the genuine distinction between the persons, which is revealed in the Bible and in Christian practice and encounter with the reality of God, but the distinctions must never lead to a suspicion that we are actually talking about three gods. Always to be avoided are modalism and tritheism, because what is at stake is the genuineness of God's self-giving to us in the incarnation and its witness, the Bible. In knowing God as Trinity, we are participating in the reality of God. When we encounter God as Trinity, it is not that God is really an undifferentiated One, so that Father, Son and Holy Spirit have no real correlation to the being of God: that would be modalism.

The doctrine of the Trinity affirms the reality of the distinctions as we encounter them: the Father and the Spirit are not incarnate; the Son reveals the Father and lives the filial life in our history; and the Holy Spirit bears witness to that and draws us into it. It is entirely appropriate for us to associate particular parts of our Christian encounter with God to particular persons of the Trinity because they are not interchangeable. But, at the same time, no one person acts without the others or separately from them. For example, the Father creates through the Son and the life-giving Spirit. The Son becomes incarnate through the Spirit to reveal the Father, and the Son's revealing work is known to us through the Spirit. What is always visible is the complex perichoresis, intertwining and interpenetration, of Unity and Trinity: each person only found through the others; each one fully and wholly God.

Our imaginations simply cannot hold the Unity and the Trinity together, and nor should we expect to. Why should we think that we could imagine God? What the Cappadocians help to provide is a defence of the reality of how God comes to us, and some language to lay out boundaries to our theology, so that we do not accidentally allow our limited imaginative capacity to make God small.

The technical language the Cappadocians give us is about the unity of God: God, Father, Son and Holy Spirit share one 'essence' or 'substance', meaning that whatever 'God' is, that is what all three persons are. When we say 'God', that is what we are talking about. They also give us language for the Threeness of God: each person of the Trinity has a distinct 'hypostasis' or 'persona'.[19] They also make the vital move to the language of 'relation' as the appropriate way to understand the names Father, Son and Holy Spirit.

Their legacy has perhaps been to emphasise the Three distinct persons of the Trinity over the One God, which was never their intention. They are concerned to take us back, over and over again, to the primary truth that there is no way of saying 'God' for Christians that is not saying 'Father, Son and Holy Spirit'. There is not first of all God, and then that God gets broken down into three aspects. This is who God is, and this is how we come to know and love God: through the truthful, self-revealing action of God by the agency of the Holy Spirit.

Questions for further thought

1. This chapter insists that Jesus does not show us a 'new' God. What do you think about that?
2. The Holy Spirit is described as the way in which we have continuing access to God's self-revelation in history, in Jesus. Does that make sense to you?
3. The Cappadocians point out that our language imports time, sequence, numbers and hierarchy into the Trinity. Try to describe their arguments and weigh them up.
4. The Cappadocians suggest that 'Father', 'Son' and 'Holy Spirit' are primarily relational terms rather than proper names. Is that a new idea to you?

3
The case for the Holy Spirit: Augustine of Hippo

While Basil, Gregory of Nyssa and Gregory of Nazianzus were using their formidable intellectual and spiritual gifts to defend the full divinity of the Son and the Holy Spirit in the eastern part of the Roman Empire of the fourth century, Augustine of Hippo was doing the same in the Latin-speaking world.

Like the Cappadocian Fathers, Augustine writes both as an outstanding thinker and as a pastor and bishop of his flock. Those are not different callings for Augustine: a bishop is called to be a teacher and guardian of the faith, and both to defend it from its opponents and to commend it to its practitioners.

Thanks to his own writing and to his impact on those who met him, Augustine comes across as a vivid, passionate, complex person driven by longings, both physical and intellectual, which find their satisfaction only in God. Highly intelligent, strongly ambitious, deeply loved, admired and imitated by his friends, Augustine was a doughty opponent and a constant advocate for the grace of God as the only source of hope, and his work on the doctrine of the Trinity is challenging on all levels. It is intellectually dazzling, but it also requires profound willingness to allow God to shape the whole person. What we worship shapes us and, unless it is God, deforms us. Only God can make us who we long to be.[1]

With the Cappadocians, Augustine is clear that the God of whom and to whom we speak is God, Father, Son and Holy Spirit, and that we know this to be so because of biblical witness and faithful Christian practice, rather than through our own intellectual surmises. He starts his great work, *On the Trinity*, in order to prove that 'the Trinity is the one and only and true God', and that only the mind guided by faith can come to this truth.[2] This is not the instinctive human idea of God but God's own self-gift. Left to our own imaginings, we would not come up with the idea of God as Father, Son and Holy Spirit, One and Three.

In his long and complicated discussion of the Trinity, written over many years, Augustine keeps coming back to the intractable problem of how human beings can speak of and worship God faithfully and truthfully while acknowledging, without fear, that our language and imaginations cannot encompass the full nature of God. In particular, we struggle to do justice to the revealed distinctions in God, Father, Son and Holy Spirit without descending into tritheism, failing to trust what we know. Our language pushes us, over and over again, to emphasise either the Oneness of God, undermining the revelation of God as Father, Son and Holy Spirit, or the Threeness of God, undermining God's self-revelation as the One God. As Augustine says, 'But, in my words, the Father, Son, and Holy Spirit are separated, and cannot be named at once, and occupy their proper places separately.'[3] We cannot name three things simultaneously.

The arguments

1 Traces of the Trinity

Famously, Augustine uses examples from our own human processing faculties to try to drive home the notion that something can be both three and one, and how we might begin to see that something can be of 'one substance' and yet have genuine distinctions. One example he uses is of our own process of acquiring knowledge. When we know things, we have to remember what we know and then decide to name that knowledge in order to use it. Augustine calls this 'memory, intellect and will'.[4] But even as we name the three things, we know that they are not separate, and that all are involved, even in the naming of them, and that all of them are internal to us.

Augustine uses these analogies for several different purposes. One, as we have already seen, is to counter those who, consciously or unconsciously, think of 'God' as a kind of 'stuff' broken into three different bits to make Father, Son and Holy Spirit. The 'bits' might all be 'god', but the impression given is that 'god' is something that is behind the three persons: first of all there is 'god', and then that gets broken down into three. Augustine's analogies are arguing that this does not have to be the case. In our own experience, we have examples of interlocking and mutually interdependent processes – memory, intellect and will, for example – that are not about something already existing and then being broken into three.[5] We also have a model that does not rely on a temporal sequence: we do not first know something, then remember it, then desire to know it; these 'operations' are simultaneous.

Augustine uses the intellectual processes as one analogy but, perhaps more helpfully, also uses the way in which love works as another. 'Behold, then, there are three things: he that loves, and that which is loved, and love.'[6] This is still examining the process of love within one human being rather than talking about love as between different people, but that is because Augustine's agenda is still to show us that we do, at least in part, see how something is Three and One, genuine unity that also has genuine distinctions.

The second way in which Augustine uses these analogies of processes within our own constitution is to point us to the way in which, whether we realise it or not, our self-knowledge reflects our being made in the image of the Trinitarian God.[7] As the human mind endlessly seeks to remember itself, to understand itself (which it cannot do without remembering) and to love itself (which it cannot do without the other two), it is being, however feebly, Trinitarian. Our capacity to remember, understand and love ourselves is also what enables us to turn that same process on others, learning to love them with the same Trinitarian process of memory and understanding. And all of this echoes in us the God in whose image we are made. When we come to love God, our own processes of self-love and love of neighbour are renewed by contact with the source, 'by partaking of whom that image not only exists, but is also renewed so as to be no longer old, and restored so as to be no longer defaced, and beatified so as to be no longer unhappy.'[8]

This search for what are sometimes called 'vestiges' or 'traces' of the Trinity in human beings is not just an intellectual exercise in Augustine's theology; it is part of God's gracious and salvific work in us: as we know ourselves more and more deeply, we are renewed more and more in the image of God, who is our life and health. Augustine's theology of self-love and self-knowledge as gifts of God that liberate us for God and for one another is surprisingly affirming of longing and desire. Most of the things we long for cannot ultimately satisfy and so have to be renewed frequently: we long for food, but soon after eating, we are back to a state of longing. But God and God's gifts can be held, and they grow rather than fade. When we love goodness, for example, we possess it, even as we grow in it.[9] If we were to cease to long for goodness and for the gifts of God, and to forget these 'hints' of the Trinitarian image of God in us so completely that the memory cannot even be revived in us at all, then we die, because life is also a gift of God.[10]

2 The eternity of God

Like the Cappadocians, Augustine is also trying to steer our imaginations away from notions of before and after and hierarchy in the Trinity, despite the biblical language of begetting and sending. His starting point is that, in all things, Father, Son and Holy Spirit work inseparably. Our encounters with God are never with just one of the Three but always with the wholeness of God. There is not 'more' of God when we invoke all three persons or 'less' of God when we speak of just one, because those are terms that belong in space and time, not in God's eternal reality.[11] Augustine argues, as the Cappadocians do, that the terms 'Father', 'Son' and 'Holy Spirit' are about relation but do not imply any change in the being of God; each is equally and unchangeably God, though each is also equally and unchangeably distinct. Augustine also uses the language of 'relation' to describe what happens between God and us. As we encounter God and become children of God, God becomes our Father, which is a transformative change for us but does not change God's eternal fatherhood, which is not dependent on us.[12]

The Son, the Word of God, has a very particular relation with human beings, since the Son takes on humanity in the incarnation. But again, Augustine argues, that changes us, not God. The Son is still 'outside' time and space, together with the Father and the Spirit, even while 'inside' it in the life of Jesus. God's knowledge and understanding of creation and of humanity do not change as the Word becomes flesh, because God, Father, Son and Holy Spirit make and sustain all things, and all things are held in God beyond the sequential way in which we live our lives as created beings.

And though the Son has one unvarying association with creation, through taking on humanity in this complete way, the Father and Spirit are not outside creation, unable to act within it. Augustine quotes scriptural examples to make his point: the voice of the Father is heard at the baptism of Jesus; the Holy Spirit is seen as a dove and as tongues of fire.[13] God has always had God's own way of presence in what God has made, enabling us, God's creatures, to encounter God in the ways that are appropriate for us. What happens in time, in history, is real and is really an encounter with God, but it is time-bound creatures who are changed by this, not the eternal God. The Son comes to us as the one who is fully God and fully human, and the Spirit gives us the Son's gift of calling the Father 'Abba', and those are genuine insights into the reality of God. At the same time, Augustine argues, the whole Trinity is at work in each manifestation of God, not just the 'person' we think we are encountering, because they are not separable.

Augustine is a fully Trinitarian Christian, not a modalist or a tritheist. But his characteristic emphasis is on the Oneness of God. Unless Scripture specifically mentions Father, Son or Holy Spirit, we should assume that references to God always mean all persons together. Likewise, we should never assume the absence of the other persons when we encounter one. Our salvation is won by God, Father, Son and Holy Spirit, not just by the Word, the Son.

3 The Holy Spirit: communion, love, gift

In this emphasis on the unity of God, the Holy Spirit plays a very particular role in Augustine's theology. Augustine notes that the name by which we know the Spirit is about the nature of God: God is spirit, God is holy. This is not to depersonalise the Holy Spirit or to take away the Spirit's particularity; on the contrary, Augustine argues, it tells us something about the role of the Holy Spirit in the life of God.

The Holy Spirit is the communion, the unity, of God. This is so strong and constitutive that the Holy Spirit is genuinely person, not just effect. Augustine's three characteristic definitions of the Holy Spirit – as communion, as gift and as love – are all interrelated and all suggest that the Holy Spirit is, in some important sense, the 'carrier' of the character of God. The most fundamental biblical description of God is that God is love. For this to be true, God must be love in God's own being, otherwise God's loving nature would be latent until God created something to love. But God who is Father, Son and Holy Spirit is already, in all eternity, self-giving and self-receiving love. When Augustine searches for human analogies to the Trinity, he describes the lover, the beloved and the love between them. To love another is to give and receive yourself to them and from them and to enable them to do the same. Love and communion or unity, therefore, are intertwined.

Since our ability to love is one of the clues that God gives us to the divine nature, it is to be expected that our experience of giving ourselves in love to another and receiving love from the other is one of those 'traces' of the Trinity that give us an insight into the loving communion of Father, Son and Holy Spirit in which the Holy Spirit may be seen as the love between the Father and the Son. Since to love and to be loved is always a matter of giving and receiving, the Holy Spirit is also gift, given between the Father and the Son.

In this, as in all our speech regarding the Trinity, Augustine warns us about the limitations imposed by our language and understanding. To say that the Holy Spirit is love, gift and communion is not to say that, without the Holy Spirit, the Father and the Son are not loving, giving and united, because there is no God 'without' all three. There is also no 'before' in God: there is never a time when the Father is not the Father of the Son, united in love and gift by the Holy Spirit. When we say 'God' this is the God we mean.

Augustine does not choose these descriptions of the Holy Spirit arbitrarily; they are dictated by scriptural witness and by Christian practice. The Holy Spirit is given to us as gift and enabler of gifts. The classic New Testament exposition of this is in 1 Corinthians 12, where Paul is trying to help the Corinthian Christians to see that the powerful gifts they so relish – like miraculous powers, healing and prophecy – are not different in kind or more important than the less flamboyant gifts. They all have the same source in the Holy Spirit and they all serve the same purpose, which is to unite and equip the body of believers. That is why chapter 12 is logically followed by Paul's great hymn to love in chapter 13. This is precisely the Trinitarian logic that Augustine is unravelling. The gift of the Holy Spirit is the gift of unifying love, which is the gift of God's own being. God is love. What the Holy Spirit gives us is always God, since that is what the Holy Spirit is. Attempting to exercise the gifts of the Spirit without unifying love is a nonsense that undoes the whole purpose and meaning of the gifts themselves, trying to make them possessions exercised for personal gain, which means that they lose the very nature of 'gift'. A gift is always a token of the one who gives it; it always carries with it the imprint of the love from which it comes, and the one who receives a gift receives that love, which draws them close to the giver.

Augustine's insight that the Holy Spirit is the one who carries the character of God is also founded in a reading of the New Testament and of Christian experience. Both in Jesus' prayer in John 14–17 and in Acts, the Holy Spirit enables Christians to know and to witness to Jesus, the Son, who reveals the Father. In John, the Holy Spirit 'teaches' and 'reminds' disciples of who Jesus is (John 14:26), so that they can be brought into the unity of love that is between the Father and the Son (17:20–26). Precisely that interconnected web of love, unity and gift is at work here, in the coming of the Holy Spirit.

In Acts, the Holy Spirit comes upon the small group of believers in tongues of fire, and suddenly they are able to communicate with the crowds in many different languages, witnessing to God and God's work through Jesus. As Peter ends his great rallying call, he exhorts his listeners to be baptised in the name of Jesus and to receive the gift of the Spirit (Acts 2:38–39), and what follows is a company of people united in love. Those who hear Peter and receive the gift of the Spirit do not just return to their previous way of life feeling a bit cosier; they are joined together in a new unity of love and purpose.

The characteristic work of the Holy Spirit is this three-faceted action of gift, love and unity, or love, unity and gift, or any order or combination of the three, in which the nature and purpose of God is displayed as invitation. We are invited into the love between the Father and the Son; this is the love that the Father gives us as the Son becomes human to draw us into it; this is the love that the Holy Spirit has 'shed abroad in our hearts' (Romans 5:5 KJV), which is nothing less than God's own self-gift. The Holy Spirit is our access to this reality, just as the Son is its revelation and enaction in time.

Augustine is reading back, then, from our encounter with the Holy Spirit into the eternal life of God, Father, Son and Holy Spirit. We encounter the Holy Spirit as the one who draws us into the love between the Father and the Son, making us one with one another and with God. In doing this, the Holy Spirit is 'doing God', in God's fullness, because what we receive is God, Father, Son and Holy Spirit, never just Son, never just Holy Spirit.

The reality of the God whom we encounter as loving and uniting gift gives us our character, too. This God is the one who calls us into being and invites us into new life. Finding 'traces' of the Trinity is key to understanding ourselves, our relationships, our world and our purpose. In Augustine's time, as in ours, the Church was full of bitter divisions, often arising out of the years of persecution that the Church had suffered before the fourth century and the conversion of the first Christian emperor. Augustine was a formidable opponent of what he saw as poor theology, but that was because of the unbreakable link that he saw between how we live and think and how we are able to testify to God. Just as Paul argues, in 1 Corinthians, that divisions among Christians are a misunderstanding of the gifts of the Spirit, so Augustine, too, argues that church divisions are a form of faithlessness. They conceal from us the reality of God, who can only be found as we throw ourselves into longing to receive God's unifying gift of love, the Holy Spirit.

4 The 'person' of the Holy Spirit

Augustine is regularly accused of making the Holy Spirit appear less personal than the Father and the Son. The Holy Spirit does not have 'characteristics' that are not shared by the other two persons; the Holy Spirit is described as holding the whole character of God – who is holy and spirit and love and gift and Oneness – rather than seeming to have a particular relationship as the Father and the Son seem to. The Holy Spirit is spoken of as what lies between the Father and the Son and unites them in self-giving love. The Holy Spirit is the love that the Son gives the Father and the Father gives the Son. The Holy Spirit is the gift that the Father gives the Son and the Son gives the Father, which is love. The Holy Spirit is the inexpressible communion of gift and love, the unity, between the Father and the Son. And all of this does make the Holy Spirit sound like some kind of impersonal force.

It is perhaps inevitable that our imaginations struggle to find the personhood of the Holy Spirit, because we do not have an earthly relationship called 'Holy Spirit'. We think that we know what 'Father' and 'Son' mean, and we see that relationship lived out in history in Jesus, the Son of the Father. But Trinitarian theology and the inclusion of the Holy Spirit in this image might force us to look more carefully at what it is for Jesus to be the Son of the Father, and to live that eternal life in the reality of history. If that is what the Holy Spirit is inviting us into, it is very different from any relationship that we experience 'naturally'.

We also do not think of our love for one another and for God as something distinct from ourselves. But again, the presence of the Holy Spirit might drive us to be more truthful about what love actually is and how transformative and costly it is. It is not just a nice feeling, or something that adds to our sense of well-being, but a genuine call to give and receive ourselves in relationship. This kind of love does not choose how loving it will be or decide for itself where it would like the boundaries to be. It is allowing self-definition to be a mutual gift. To see this process as showing us the 'character' of God, at work through the Holy Spirit, might be an important clue about the nature and purpose of the Church, as we shall see when we come to look at the Creed's declaration of faith in the Church. This is the human, time-bound, historical living out of the Holy Spirit's gift of the character of God, Father, Son and Holy Spirit, lover, beloved and the love between them; communion of gift and reciprocity.

That might still leave us feeling that the Holy Spirit does not have a 'face', but it might also make us begin to realise that this is because we do not yet have our own 'faces'. It is not just God that we can only see in a mirror darkly but ourselves, because the two are inseparable.

Questions for further thought

1 Do you instinctively think of God as Three or as One?
2 Augustine connects truthful knowledge of ourselves with the search for truthful knowledge of God. Is this a helpful connection?

3 Augustine argues that we never encounter one 'person' of the Trinity without the others also being present. Does that tie in with your experience?
4 Augustine's description of the Holy Spirit as gift, unity and bond of love has been accused of making the Holy Spirit an impersonal force rather than a 'person'. Do you agree? How would you want to describe the Holy Spirit?

4
The Holy Spirit defended: summarising the arguments

The Cappadocians and Augustine came from different parts of the Christian Roman Empire, speaking different languages and facing different challenges. They helped to forge the language and imagination of the Christian Church at a key moment in its development, in the fourth century.

The defence that they and others make for the Creed's declaration of the full divinity of the Son and the Spirit forms all responses since. If God is not like this – One God, who is Father, Son and Holy Spirit – then the world is not the creation of love, and the Church is not the company of all humanity, called to share the good news that God invites us into new life.

The arguments

1 Bible

In arguing the case that the Holy Spirit, like the Son, is God, and that there is no God who is not *this* God, both the Cappadocians and Augustine draw on Scripture and on Christian practice, because they are not putting together an intellectually stimulating set of ideas but trying to be faithful to how God has been revealed to us. They quote Scripture extensively, and they argue that this description of God is the only one that makes sense of the whole sweep of the Bible, read through the lens of the coming of Jesus Christ. Other cases can be made by using the occasional text on its own, but only this understanding of God, Father, Son and Holy Spirit, One God, enables all that is said about God to be accommodated in creedal language.

Similarly, Augustine and the Cappadocians read the reality of God from Christian practice. We baptise in the threefold name of God, as the source of forgiveness, renewal and new life. In the Eucharist, the Holy Communion, we acknowledge the death of Christ as the work of God for our salvation. In the ordering of the Church, we rely on the Holy Spirit to give gifts of ordination to keep our witness truthful and faithful, grounded in Scripture and sacraments. We assume that our communal life as Church is not an optional extra to an essentially private faith but a witness to the new creation, constantly forgiven, renewed by the same God who created from nothing and holds all life in being. Our practice tells us what we believe: that God is One, and is Father, Son and Holy Spirit.

2 Language

The Cappadocians and Augustine both suggest that those who do not read the Bible and Christian practice as revelatory of God's Trinitarian reality are misunderstanding the difference between God and us. To know God as Father, Son and Holy Spirit is to know as truly as we can because it is how God has shown the divine being to us; but that is not to know everything there is to know about God or to be able to express fully even what we experience of God.

In particular, these theologians suggest that we mislead ourselves with language that imports time and hierarchy into the Trinitarian life of God because they are unavoidably part of our lived experience. But God is not a created being; God is the Creator of time, not its creature, and God, Father, Son and Holy Spirit are wholly One and equal, with no person more or less God than the others.

The Holy Spirit defended

It is the language of 'begotten' and of 'proceeding' and of being 'sent' that particularly sets up the temptation to false readings. John's Gospel says that the Son is 'begotten' from the Father (John 1:14 NKJV). If that was being said in a human context, it would mean that first of all there was the Father and then came the Son. But John's Gospel itself sets parameters around that idea by saying that the Son, the Word, is both with God from the beginning and is also God (1:1–2), warning us that the language is being twisted into new shapes to try to enable an enormous idea.

Carefully, then, the developing language of the Creed, as spelled out by the theologians we have been examining, insists that there is not first of all God, who then becomes Father, Son and Holy Spirit by some divine process. Through all eternity, God is Father, Son and Holy Spirit.

Furthermore, imagining a sequential process in God – in which first of all there is the Father and then the Father decides to bring the Son and the Spirit into existence – makes space for notions of hierarchy. The Father is 'really' God, all alone, while the other two are lesser, dependent beings, however much they are beloved and willed by the Father. This impression is further reinforced since the Son and the Spirit are said to be 'sent', so that our encounter with them in the realms of time and history seems to be at the bidding of the Father, who does not himself get involved in the messy world of creation.

As with the other attempts at defining God that are ruled out by the Creed's summary, this notion of Son and Spirit as sent does have a biblical underpinning but only if read with the kind of eyes that see mutuality as impossible. Although the Son and the Spirit are sent, they are not minions, and their mission (the word means 'sending') is not foisted upon them. Each person of the Trinity enables the witness to the whole reality of God. The Son reveals the Father, and the Spirit gives the Son's relationship to the Father to us, the Son's sisters and brothers. The Father is 'dependent' upon the Son for God's 'fatherly' nature: without the Son, God is not Father. The Holy Spirit defines the holiness and uncreatedness of God: God is holy and spirit. The Son is 'dependent' on the Holy Spirit to continue to hold the filial relationship of Son to Father, of humanity in Christ to Father, through time. The Holy Spirit comes upon Mary to bring the Son into humanity; the Father and the Spirit confirm the person and mission of the Son at baptism. The mutual revelation and authorisation is inescapable throughout the biblical witness to the incarnation.[1]

Another indication of the instinctive hierarchical and sequential thinking that is brought to Trinitarian theology from our own imaginations is the way in which the different language about the 'origins' of the Son and Spirit are construed. The Son is described as 'begotten', while the Spirit is described as 'proceeding'. Once it is accepted that to speak of the Son as begotten does not imply there was a time 'before' the Son's existence – when God was alone, undifferentiated and not Father – and does not imply any parallel with the way in which children come into existence in human experience, then the fight moves on to the Holy Spirit. Why is the Holy Spirit not also 'begotten'? Surely it is better to be 'Son' and 'begotten' than to be 'Holy Spirit' and 'proceed'? Surely the language implies a deeper likeness and intimacy between Son and Father than between Father and Holy Spirit?

We will return to this issue when we look at each of the statements the Creed makes about the Holy Spirit. In John 15:26, Jesus speaks of the coming of the Counsellor, the Advocate, the Spirit of Truth, who 'proceeds' or 'comes forth' from the Father. This, too, is an eternal reality. Just as God does not become Father and Son, so God does not become Holy Spirit. But for Augustine and the Cappadocians, the difference in the language used is a vital pointer to the real distinctions within the Trinity. The Holy Spirit is not a second Son and does not secretly long to be. Reading back from how we encounter God into the eternal reality of God, we see that it is only the Son who becomes incarnate, and it is the Holy Spirit who enables the incarnation, and prays in us, 'Abba, Father,' holding the relationship between Son and Father in our reality for our salvation. Self-centred as we are, we assume that for the Son to become like us is the main point of the incarnation, and therefore that the work of the Son is more significant than any other. But the life of faith enabled by the Holy Spirit suggests that the point of the incarnation is for us to become like the Son, through the gift of the Spirit, and that the whole work of the wholeness of God directed towards us is vital for us. We cannot live from just one 'person' of the Trinity.

We can only use the language we have, knowing its inadequacy. But the way in which language is used accrues meaning. Words do not stay in one place. The language we use about the Trinity has the potential gently, but insistently, to undermine what it seems to imply about hierarchy and about how God can relate to time and history.

3 Persons and relations

Another area in which Augustine and the Cappadocians help to clarify Trinitarian theology is by bringing greater definition to how to distinguish Father, Son and Holy Spirit without undermining the unity of God.

Father, Son and Holy Spirit are not three 'substances'; they are One God. But the distinctions between them are genuinely part of the reality of God, not just the way we happen to experience God's action. On the contrary, we experience God's action like this because this is how God is.

Both the Cappadocians and Augustine use the notion of 'relation' as a way of bypassing our assumption that if God has three names, there must be three gods, or, at the very least, three pieces of God. The Cappadocians argue that a relation is not an action, requiring a before and after, and it is not a substance, suggesting a thing separate from the one who holds it. The Father is not the Father's 'name', while the Son and the Spirit have different 'names'. Each comes from the relation in which they stand to one another, which is entirely one of self-giving and self-receiving. Augustine, in particular, uses a whole range of analogies to show how we have threefold operational relations within our own experience of how we function, without that making us people divided into different parts. Memory, understanding and will are distinct, and yet none can operate without the others, and none is separated from the others.

As Augustine ruefully acknowledges, the more this theology of Unity and Threeness gets translated, the more it leads to misunderstanding.[2] He writes in Latin and the Cappadocians write in Greek, and both are trying to give shape to the question 'Three what and one what?' in a way that preserves the reality of both. We simply cannot do that and do not have any words that will enable something so far outside our own human experience. Augustine's 'traces' of the Trinity in us emphasise the Oneness at the expense of the real distinctions, however much he battles against that, which is why he is careful to say that these are not 'descriptions' of the Trinity but hints and imaginative aids.

What Father, Son and Holy Spirit have in common is 'substance' or 'essence' or 'godness', but that does not lie behind the Threeness, as though it could be accessed independently of the Father, Son and Holy Spirit. 'Godness' is always Trinity. What distinguishes the Father, Son and Holy Spirit is called *hypostasis* in Greek and *persona* in Latin, but their distinction is not separation.

In English, the word 'person' has particular dangers when we assume that we know what a 'person' is, bringing individuality and personal consciousness overtones to the discussion of the Trinity. But the Trinity are not three different people, not even three different people who get on particularly well, cooperate in all things, and tag-team brilliantly and instinctively. The Trinity are One, as no human persons are one with another, however close. The Trinity do not share 'godness' in the way that we share 'humanity'; the Trinity are God.

There is no perfect solution to this. The language of 'persons' and 'relations' developed for this purpose in the fourth century is helpful, and it is the best we can do. But to be aware of the impossible task the language is undertaking is to be more properly cautious about how we apply it. We cannot let it prevent us from venturing to speak of God, Father, Son and Holy Spirit, but we can be careful to keep attempting to hold Oneness and Threeness in creative tension.

Perhaps the heart of our own longing to love and be loved, to be known but still mysterious and to be united with others without losing our own personality gives us some window into why this discussion is so important. God is a unity so profound that nothing can break God apart; yet this unity is full of the joy of distinction, where Father, Son and Holy Spirit are not interchangeable but are only who they are because of the other two. In God, Oneness and Threeness do not have to be different states, for in God, they are God's being.

We cannot simply read a prescription for Church and society out of the character of God the Holy Trinity, tempting as it is. But we can, to some extent, see our own growth in personal and communal discipleship as being measured by whether it makes it harder or easier for us to long for God in God's fullness. Our choices, actions and relationships can bring us nearer to a space where we trust each other to help us to become who we are – together, not separately – where to be a person does not mean battling for our own individuality over against that of others, where we might be able to make space for difference as gift, not a problem. None of this will make us godlike, and none of this is achievable, or even something we might desire, without the presence and action of God the Holy Spirit breathing our filial reality into us, sisters and brothers of the Son, and so sisters and brothers to one another, receiving ourselves from the Father 'from whom every family in heaven and on earth takes its name' (Ephesians 3:15).

The Cappadocians and Augustine are by no means the only theologians who have helped to make a case for the full divinity of the Holy Spirit, but they are helpfully representative in bringing out some of the issues that come up when doing Trinitarian theology. With the help of the kind of ground-clearing they have done, we will now look directly at what the Creed says 'we believe' about the Holy Spirit.

Questions for further thought

1 What do you consider to be the positive and negative things about thinking of Father, Son and Holy Spirit as 'persons'?
2 The Cappadocians and Augustine argue that the Bible and church worship only make sense if God is Father, Son and Holy Spirit. Do you agree?
3 Do you instinctively think of one person of the Trinity as more 'really' God than the others?
4 Do you think our own hopes and fears about loving and being loved might help us to imagine God who is Three and One?

5
The Holy Spirit in the Creed

The earliest versions of the Creed were developed in the context of baptism and worship to enable new Christians to affirm their faith and those whom they were joining to renew theirs. We have some examples of these creeds, all of which are Trinitarian.[1] They formed the basis for the more detailed Creed, developed first of all at the Council of Nicaea in 325 and then expanded over the following half-century. This Creed, too, was and is used in worship. It enables those gathered to praise God and to entrust their lives and their world to this God whom the Creed outlines.

But, as we have seen, the Nicene Creed also took on a new purpose, which was to add greater definition and unanimity to what Christians believe about God. People tried, with the best will in the world, to put forward interpretations of what the Bible tells us about the nature of God, Father, Son and Holy Spirit, and many of these interpretations proved unsuccessful in their suggestions. The primary and most pressing focus of these attempts was to define who Jesus is in relation to God, and so the earliest forms of the Nicene Creed concentrate on clarifying the conditions that must be met if we are to trust that it is really God we are meeting in Jesus.

The Creed defines the whole world as the work of God, Father, Son and Holy Spirit. Creation is a gift of the God who is already gift and giver in God's very being. God is the 'Father' of the 'Son', who comes to live with us in our humanity, and whom we know by the name of Jesus.

The declarations made about the Son and the Father as one in their divinity, though distinct in their relation, were extended with extreme brevity to the Holy Spirit. The earliest Nicene Creed, after paragraphs about the Father and the Son, simply says, 'And we believe in the Holy Spirit.' The particular theological challenge of the incarnation and its implications for our understanding of God was the primary focus of the earliest Creed of Nicaea. The Holy Spirit seemed, at first glance, more easily accommodated within existing theology than the Son who becomes human. But as Trinitarian theology developed more fully – with its insistence that God really is Three as well as One, and that the distinctions within God are eternally part of the nature of God, not just how we happen to encounter God – further work on the place of the Holy Spirit became pressing.

After the brevity of the first Nicene Creed of 325, as the writings of Augustine, the Cappadocians and others make clear, the relationship of the Holy Spirit to the Father and the Son also came under scrutiny, with various suggestions about how the Bible and church practice should be read in expounding the role of the Holy Spirit.

At that point, towards the end of the fourth century, a further paragraph was added to the Creed, expanding what it is to believe and trust in the Holy Spirit as we do the Father and the Son. This is what the Nicene Creed now says about the Holy Spirit:

> We believe in the Holy Spirit,
>   the Lord, the giver of life,
>   who proceeds from the Father (and the Son),
>   who with the Father and the Son is worshipped
>   and glorified,
>   who has spoken through the prophets.
>   We believe in one holy catholic and apostolic
>   Church.

The Holy Spirit in the Creed

We acknowledge one baptism for the forgiveness of sins.
We look for the resurrection of the dead,
and the life of the world to come.

Each phrase is carefully chosen and has its basis both in the Bible and in Christian practice. In this chapter, we will go through these affirmations to help us to build up a fuller picture of the Creed's theology of the Holy Spirit.

The Lord

The Creed calls the Holy Spirit 'the Lord' as a strong assertion of the Spirit's divinity. In the Hebrew Bible, 'the Lord' is the particular name for Israel's God, in a form that, though it is holy, may still be spoken. God's own great Name, revealed to Moses, is too powerful and transcendent for our use but when 'the Lord' is uttered, the resonance of God's self-naming is heard in the ways in which human beings respond. This is the Lord, the one to whom we owe all that we have and are, all our loyalty and trust. 'The Lord' distinguishes the character and particularity of this God, as opposed to the 'gods' of the surrounding nations. Israel's God is One, the only Lord, and no other claimant to the people's loyalty and devotion can be admitted. Yet, graciously, the Lord does not just demand obedience from the people but also offers to make a covenant with them, which binds God as it binds the people. God offers to be the Lord for this particular people, so that they may call upon God as one who has promised to hear. The Lord will match – indeed, wildly exceed – the faithfulness of the people; they will be able to trust in the Lord, who has made this promise to them to be their God, and they will be given, as surety, the divine Name.

As part of that covenant of faithfulness, the Lord gives Israel the Law, which serves the twofold purpose of revealing the character of God and making the people into a new and holy nation living in accordance with the reality of God. In time, the Lord also promises to be present and available, not exclusively, but reliably, in the Temple.

At the heart of this lies the Lord's willingness to be known truly and to be faithful to this human community for their good, not out of any need on God's part.

This is what makes it so striking when that title is given to Jesus. Particularly powerful is Thomas's declaration of faith to the risen Jesus, 'My Lord and my God!' (John 20:28). Jesus' followers are seeing the Lord, who has never been far from the people but who has now come even closer, living and dying in faithful commitment to keep the covenant of self-giving love.

The simple statement in the Creed that we believe in the Holy Spirit as Lord is acknowledging that the Holy Spirit, too, is God, drawing close to the people and making a covenant of faithful grace with them. When God names God to Moses, the Name encompasses the Holy Spirit: the Holy Spirit is Lord; the Lord is Father, Son and Holy Spirit.

In the New Testament, the Holy Spirit is the one who enables us to see that Jesus is Lord at every stage of Jesus' earthly life from conception through to resurrection. Paul declares, 'No one can say, "Jesus is Lord", except by the Holy Spirit' (1 Corinthians 12:3). The work of the Holy Spirit enables us to see and to experience the 'lordship' of Jesus Christ as the action of the same Lord who has been made known throughout history, and who has always reached out for and drawn near to the people. The Holy Spirit highlights the 'character' of the Lord in Jesus Christ.

It is no surprise that many of the references to the Holy Spirit as Lord and God are also in Paul's correspondence with the

Corinthian church. They seem to have been very interested in the showy gifts of the Spirit but to have needed some guidance to see that these are part of God's ongoing shaping of a people who can live from and display God's own character. Speaking in tongues, prophecy, healing and miracles make no sense unless they are part of a growing faith in God who is, most fundamentally, love (1 Corinthians 12—13).

Paul starts 1 Corinthians with an exposition of the 'foolishness' of God, which can only begin to be discovered as wisdom through the interpretation of the Spirit. God's wisdom is 'secret and hidden' (1 Corinthians 2:7), only comprehended and therefore only revealed by the Spirit (2:10—13). Only the Spirit can enable us to understand the gifts that God gives. The interpretive role of the Spirit is highlighted in a slightly different context in 2 Corinthians 3:12—18. Paul is again making the point that only the Spirit who is Lord and God can bring us close to God. When Moses had been close to God, Paul argues, the people could only look at Moses when he was wearing a veil because Moses could not truly and naturally mediate the glory of God, since it was not his own. But the glory of God is the Spirit's own glory, and so the Spirit is able to make us free for God's glory, not mediated through another veiled human being but glowing from the source of all glory: the fullness of God. Paul very deliberately calls the Spirit 'the Lord' several times in this passage to drive home the message: only God can reveal God, and since that is what the Spirit does, the Spirit is Lord, too.

Paul also uses Temple imagery about the Spirit (1 Corinthians 3:16). In the Hebrew Scriptures, the Lord had promised to be present when the people prayed in the Temple, and now the Lord has come even closer and promises to be present in each one of us as we become the people with whom the Lord dwells and in whom the character and faithfulness of the Lord are displayed. 'God's Spirit dwells in you,' Paul declares, picking up on all those echoes of the covenant between God and the people with the Temple at the heart of them. Now, we are the Temple.

These two aspects of the Spirit's role – as the one who is able to interpret God's character for us, because the Spirit is God, and as the one who is the gracious, ongoing, faithful and challenging presence of God with us – are key in a number of New Testament passages. Jesus' long expository prayer before his death (John 14–17) is full of references to the Spirit's witnessing and convicting presence; in Acts, the Holy Spirit leads and guides and encourages the witness of the newly fledged Christian missionary movement; in 1 Peter 4:14, the Spirit enables the persecuted Christians to know that they are sharing in the glory of God and not to doubt the faithfulness of God, even in suffering; in Revelation, the Spirit speaks to the churches and guides the visions of the author, giving warnings and encouragement in trials.

In all of this, the Spirit is the Lord. The Spirit ministers from the Spirit's own divinity, witnessing always to the shared reality of God, Father, Son and Holy Spirit. The lordship of the Spirit witnesses to and continuously upholds and re-establishes the lordship of God, who is Trinity.

The Giver of Life

As the priest and deacon stand before the Holy Doors, in the liturgy of St John Chrysostom, they say:

> Heavenly King, Consoler, the Spirit of Truth, present in all places and filling all things, the Treasury of blessings and the Giver of life, come O Good One, and dwell in us, cleanse us of all stain and save our souls.[2]

This beautiful, complex web of ideas helps an understanding of why the Creed calls the Spirit the Giver of Life. Both in holding all creation in being and in enabling new life in Christ, the Spirit is appropriately described as the source of life.

The description unites the Spirit with the Father and the Son in bringing creation into being. It is easy to hear the start of the Creed as saying that only the 'Father Almighty' is the 'maker of heaven and earth'. But it follows this up in the declaration about the full divinity of the Son by saying that through the Son 'all things were made'. As with all the creedal statements, this is a succinct summary of what the New Testament says: John 1:1–4, in particular, states with absolute clarity that all things that are not God come into being through the Word who is God. The Creed strongly affirms the principle that all the persons of the Trinity are involved in all the works of God. The Father does not create without the Son and the Spirit, because they are all One God, the source of all that is.

> For the first principle of existing things is One, creating through the Son and perfecting through the Spirit . . . You are therefore to perceive three, the Lord who gives the order, the Word who creates, and the Spirit who confirms.[3]

The Holy Spirit's active role in creation is seen in Genesis 1:2, where the Spirit hovers over the waters. Breath and Word, Spirit and Son, are involved in the 'speaking' of creation into being. Similarly, the Breath of God is given to the human creature in Genesis 2:7 to make the earthling a living being.[4] While the 'breathed word' is essential to all creation, the earthling receives the Breath of God directly because this creature has a particular responsibility for 'imaging' God in creation. The debate about quite what this means is endless, but it is given an illuminating focus by the New Testament, which declares that the Son is the primary 'image-bearer'. Colossians 1:15–16 says, 'He is the image of the invisible God, the firstborn of all creation; for in him all things in heaven and on earth were created.' Just as the opening of John's Gospel is a retelling of the creation narrative, 'in the beginning' in the light of Christ, so, too, is the statement in Colossians. It deliberately picks up and reinterprets the 'image' language of Genesis 1:26–27.

That opens up a dazzling insight into the interaction of Son and Spirit in the work of creation. The Spirit is breathed into the human creature so that it may receive the image of the Son through whom all things were made. In time, in history, the Son comes to inhabit that image directly, to remake it from the inside. We tend to think that the Son becomes incarnate in order to be like us and to learn what it is to be human, but it is actually the other way round. Human beings are made in the image of the Son through the life-giving power of the Spirit but have lost the ability to live in that profound gift of God. The Son comes to restore it, to take it home again, to fill it with divine life and breath again. Christian discipleship is an invitation to become again 'the image of God' by becoming the body of the Son, the body of Christ.

Just as the Holy Spirit breathes through creation 'in the beginning', so the Holy Spirit is the life-giver in this reclamation project. It is through the Holy Spirit, Luke says, that the Son of God will become human, in Jesus (Luke 1:35). Just as the Spirit hovers over the waters of creation, so the Holy Spirit hovers over Mary in this act of re-creation. Later, the Holy Spirit hovers over the waters of Jesus' baptism as a dove. The echoes of creation resonate throughout this narrative of re-creation.

When the risen Jesus breathes upon his disciples, he says, 'Receive the Holy Spirit' (John 20:22), giving such a powerful image of the inseparable recreating work of Son and Spirit. Jesus' work of restoring the 'image of the invisible God' is now breathed onto the disciples sent out to witness to the Son of the Father, in the power of the Spirit.

Ezekiel the prophet is taken by the Spirit to a valley full of dry bones (Ezekiel 37) and told to prophesy to them. They represent God's people, who have lost all hope, all belief in the future, all trust in God. But when Ezekiel obeys, he sees the bones being covered with flesh as he speaks what he is told to speak. Through the prophet Ezekiel, the Lord, the faithful One, promises to open the graves. 'I will put my Spirit in you,' the Lord declares, just as 'in the beginning'. In John's telling of the resurrection encounter with Jesus, the grave has been opened, and the risen Jesus stands with his disciples again and breathes the Holy Spirit upon them.

The Creed's avowal of the Holy Spirit as Giver of Life rests on this tightly interwoven testimony to the Spirit as the source of life 'in the beginning', throughout life, in every breath and in the new creation. It is the Spirit who raises Jesus from the dead (1 Peter 3:18; Romans 8:11) and who will also give new life to us in the daily renewing of the 'image' of the Son in us and at the final resurrection.

The Holy Spirit proceeds from the Father (and/with) the Son

The Holy Spirit is described in John's Gospel as 'proceeding' or 'coming forth' or 'going out' from the Father (John 15:26). Throughout the great prayer of Jesus in John 14–17, there is a continuous interplay of ideas about the Holy Spirit as the One who enables the continuing witness to and trust in Jesus after his death and resurrection. Jesus' prayer is that his followers will be enabled to live from and testify to the unity between Jesus and the Father, and that this will be the ongoing gift of the Holy Spirit.

When we say these words in the Creed, we are part of that testimony: God is Father, Son and Holy Spirit, unbroken loving unity, we declare. This is what 'we believe'.

In its original form, the Creed used the description in John 15:26, that the Holy Spirit proceeds from the Father. For Orthodox theology, following on from the groundbreaking Trinitarian work of the Cappadocians, the 'monarchia' of the Father is a key idea.[5] 'God' is personal through and through; we must not conceive of 'God' first and then imagine this divine substance broken up into the three 'persons'. Instead, the best our language and imaginations can do is to picture the Father as the 'source' from whom the Son is 'begotten' and the Spirit 'proceeds'. We have already seen the careful boundaries put around this by the Cappadocian Fathers. There is no sequence or time in the way in which Son and Spirit relate to the Father. There is never just the Father: God is always Father, Son and Holy Spirit. But to ensure that we never imagine divinity in the abstract, the Bible gives us the language of 'begotten' and 'proceeding'.

This language also ensures the distinctiveness of the three persons. The Spirit is not the Son and so is not 'begotten'. Nonetheless, the Spirit's 'procession' is from the fatherliness of God, the self-giving reality of the Father, who is known only through the Son and the Spirit. Both are sent to us to draw us to our own source in the fatherliness of God, only made possible to us through the Holy Spirit who unites us with the Son. The Spirit is not 'the image of the invisible God' – only the Son becomes a human being. But the Spirit breathes the life of the Son into us, and prays the words of the Son in us, to share that life-giving relationship between God and humanity, made real for us in Jesus, 'enfleshed' for us by the Spirit.

That does not mean that the Son and the Spirit are less God than the Father, or in any way subordinate. It is necessary to keep circling back to the reality that all of God is involved in all of God's actions towards us. The Son and the Spirit are as much their own senders to us as the Father. The 'sending' of the Son and the Spirit is for us, and it changes nothing in the unbroken relationship of God in God's own eternity.

In the Western form of the Creed, however, the Holy Spirit is said to proceed 'from the Father and the Son'.[6] This, too, has biblical precedent. In John 16:7, Jesus says that he will send the Holy Spirit; Galatians 4:6 calls the Spirit 'the Spirit of his Son', as do other biblical texts. Underlying this is the witness of the New Testament and of church practice and discipleship, that the Spirit's work is always associated with making and remaking the filial image in humanity; in other words, that the Spirit's work is always 'Son-shaped'.

But the problem is that the unity of action between the Father and the Son in relation to the Spirit can undermine the overall unity between the three persons, and the relational distinctiveness of the Three. The language can suggest that the Father and the Son are 'really' God, and the Spirit is subordinate; it also clouds the distinct, untransferable way in which the Son and the Spirit relate to the Father, the 'source'.

The continuing opposition to what is called the filioque clause – *filioque* is the Latin for 'and the Son' – is both about doctrine and about the use and misuse of power. The Nicene Creed and its earliest developments, which did not contain the 'filioque', were agreed by ecumenical councils, which contained representatives from Eastern and Western Christians, whereas the filioque clause was added without consultation by the Western churches alone. Mistrust between Christians is not a modern phenomenon, but it is a costly one, as this controversy was one of the causes of the great schism between East and West that continues to this day.

The Creed's intention in speaking of the procession of the Spirit is to declare the full divinity of the Spirit, so that we trust that the Spirit's action is the action of God for us. It is also to assert the full 'personhood' of the Spirit, who is not another form of the Son but fully personal and relational in encounter with us, as God always is.

With the Father and the Son he is worshipped and glorified[7]

We have already seen that Augustine and the Cappadocian Fathers saw the Holy Spirit as the means by which we are able to worship. Without the presence and action of the Holy Spirit, we cannot recognise God or offer God the true worship of created beings in the presence of their Creator, of adopted daughters and sons alongside the Son.

This clause in the Creed goes further. The Holy Spirit does not just enable us to worship the Father and the Son but, like them, is a proper recipient of our worship because the Holy Spirit, too, is God.

The great prophets of the Old Testament frequently point out the stupidity of worshipping anything that is not God. In 1 Kings 18, Elijah challenges the prophets of the god Baal to a kind of duel to demonstrate whose god is true and powerful. The prophets of Baal call upon their god and nothing happens. Elijah mocks them, saying, 'Cry aloud! Surely he is a god; either he is meditating, or he has wandered away, or he is on a journey, or perhaps he is asleep and must be awakened' (1 Kings 18:27). There is no response from Baal because Baal is no god, just a human creation. When Elijah's turn comes to call upon the Lord, the response is overwhelming, and the watching people fall on their faces, crying, 'The LORD indeed is God! The LORD indeed is God!' (18:39).

That is why the first commandment given to Moses and the Israelites is a prohibition of idols and of misusing the name of the Lord (Exodus 20:4–7). The whole character of God's people is demeaned when they turn away from God; it makes them forget who created and liberated them; it makes them forget their dependence on the faithfulness of God; it makes them forget who they are. As God sings to the people in Isaiah, 'Why do you spend your money for that which is not bread, and your labour for that which does not satisfy?' (Isaiah 55:2). God is freely offering all that the people need and yet they try to achieve by their efforts what God is offering by grace. This is the archetypal 'sin', as described in Genesis 2:5. The serpent tempts the newly created human couple with the idea that they will be 'like God', yet the bitter irony is that in creating human beings, God has already made them 'images' of God, freely giving what they now try to snatch.

To offer our worship to the true God is to return to our right minds, our rightful place at God's side. God does not need our worship in order to be God, but we need to offer our worship in order to be ourselves. Whenever a prophet is given a glimpse into heaven, what they are shown is that worship of God is at the heart of reality: Isaiah hears the seraphs calling out, 'Holy!' (Isaiah 5:3); Ezekiel sees extraordinary creatures wheeling around in worship and service of the One upon the throne (Ezekiel 1); John the Seer glimpses through the open door in heaven the worship of humans, spirits and strange living creatures, all crying, 'Holy!' (Revelation 4). At the centre of all reality, God's myriad creatures sing in praise and joy because they are in God's presence and know themselves created and redeemed in love.

Worship offered to the true God, then, is redeeming and restoring for the worshippers. It is part of the work of the Holy Spirit to bring us into worship but also to receive our worship. With the Father and the Son, the Holy Spirit creates, redeems and restores, enabling us to rejoice in our relationship with God. It is perhaps particularly appropriate that the one whom we call 'Holy' Spirit enables us to sing 'holy, holy, holy' with all God's strange and wonderful creatures.

Like the Father and the Son, the Holy Spirit is also to be glorified. Worshipping God and glorifying God belong together because God's glory is the way in which God's presence is seen. It is part of God's gracious faithfulness to creation that God's presence can be 'seen', even if mysteriously. God's glory is made manifest not for God's sake but for ours. Psalm 29 calls on the heavenly beings and all God's people to 'ascribe to the LORD the glory of his name; worship the LORD in holy splendour' (Psalm 29:2), and as the song of God's glory ascends, God's own voice rings out with terrifying and exhilarating force. As we worship, God becomes more and more present to us, not because God was absent before but because we were. In Psalm 19, all creation sings the song of God's glory in ways appropriate to their nature: 'The heavens are telling the glory of God' (Psalm 19:1).

In the Old Testament, God's glory is often visible as light and is overwhelming, as though it has a weight that makes human beings sink to the ground. When Moses has been talking to God, Moses' own face is so unbearably bright to look at that he has to veil himself in ordinary discourse with the people of God. Ezekiel marks the sad, slow withdrawal of God's glory from the Temple, as God's people turn away from God. In Ezekiel 8:4, God's glory is at the entrance of the inner court; in chapter 9, the glory of the Lord moves progressively further and further from the heart of the Temple until, by the end of chapter 11, the glory of the Lord has left the city altogether to take rest on a mountain outside the holy city. Jerusalem, and the Temple in particular, had been one of the symbols of God's faithful commitment to the people, and God promised to be present there to those who came to worship, but, as they turn away from God, so God's presence, God's glory, recedes.

In the New Testament, the notion of the glory of God is closely associated with Jesus, who is God's presence and faithfulness in a new and extraordinary way. In John's Gospel, the dazzling light of the glory of God comes into the world in Jesus, 'and we have seen his glory, the glory as of a father's only son' (John 1:14). This is the light that no darkness can extinguish or vanquish. God's glory and presence are particularly evident, in John's theology, in Jesus' suffering and death. This is where darkness tries and fails to extinguish the light; this is where we see God's faithful commitment never to remove the glory of God from us, not even in death.[8] Death cannot make God depart from us; instead, it glorifies God by bringing God's presence to us even in the places where God seems most absent.

In the Pauline Epistles, the glory of God is shared with us, the adopted children of God. For example, Romans 6:4 says that 'just as Christ was raised from the dead by the glory of the Father, so we too might walk in newness of life'; 2 Corinthians 4:6 connects God's original creation of the light with the action of that same God in Jesus, giving 'the light of the knowledge of the glory of God in the face of Jesus Christ'; 1 Thessalonians 2:12 reminds the Christians of Thessalonica that God 'calls you into his own kingdom and glory'.[9]

One of the places where the glory of God, the visible presence of God in Jesus, is directly connected with the Holy Spirit is 1 Peter 4:14. When Christians accept persecution in the name of Christ, 'the Spirit of glory' is with them. In a more extended way, Jesus' great prayer for the disciples as he faces death (John 14–17) consistently connects the coming of the Holy Spirit with presence: the disciples may fear the absence of Jesus, but Jesus reassures them that the Holy Spirit is the continuing witness and presence of God in Christ. 'He will glorify me, because he will take what is mine and declare it to you,' Jesus says (John 16:14). The Holy Spirit continues the glorious presence of God, which has come close in Jesus Christ. The fierce light of the tongues of flame at Pentecost echo the glory of God present in the pillar of fire with the Israelites on their journey through the wilderness; the Holy Spirit is the presence of God with us in baptism, as God was present with the people as they walked through the Red Sea; the gifts of the Holy Spirit come upon us as the presence and action of God. Above all, that perfecting gift of love draws us into the presence of God, Father, Son and Holy Spirit, the perfect circle of love.

In Jesus, the glory of God comes close and is visible to those who are willing to see. The Old Testament witnesses to God's gracious gift of presence, in glory, always available to those who worship; now that 'glory' becomes human to bring God's self-gift into our reality. And that ongoing self-gift of God in Christ is the Holy Spirit, the one who brings the glory of Christ to humanity in the incarnation and continues to hold that glorious image in reality in sisters and brothers of the Son, praying, 'Abba, Father.'

Just as the Holy Spirit enables our worship and receives it, so, too, the Holy Spirit enables us to glorify God and is glorified as we do so. The 'glory of God' is how we describe our awareness of God's presence, sometimes terrifying, sometimes blazing, sometimes tender, always drawing us into unity with one another and with God. That is why worship and glory go together, and the Holy Spirit is the mediator of both for us. The Holy Spirit is to be glorified in worship and in our lives together, which receive the gift of God's glorious presence, Father, Son and Holy Spirit.

He has spoken through the prophets

The role of the Holy Spirit as 'inspirer' is testified to in a number of ways in the Bible. In Luke's Gospel, at the start of his public ministry, Jesus went to his local synagogue in Nazareth and read from the prophet Isaiah: 'The Spirit of the Lord is upon

The Holy Spirit in the Creed

me, because he has anointed me to bring good news to the poor' (Luke 4:16-19, quoting Isaiah 61:1-2). Jesus declares his mission, to 'seek out and to save the lost' (Luke 19:10) as the mission given to him by the Spirit, the mission of the anointed one, the Christ. In Acts, the Spirit comes upon the disciples in tongues of fire, enabling them to speak in other languages, and Peter explains to the astonished crowd that this is a messianic sign of the new age of God's action. In the old age, only kings were anointed with the Spirit, but now, after the coming of Jesus the Christ, the Spirit will be poured out on everyone: everyone will be able to speak the words of the Lord in the name of the Lord, in the outpouring, anointing gift of the Holy Spirit (Acts 2:17-21, quoting Joel 2:28-32).

The great prophets of ancient Israel recorded their 'call' to prophesy as a sort of testimonial, and they were careful to distinguish between the words they had been given by the Lord and their words and understanding.[10] To prophesy in the name of the Lord was a serious and heavy undertaking, turning the life of a prophet upside down and setting him apart from those around him.

The promise in Joel that the gift of prophecy would fall on all marked a significant departure: God was coming so close that the privilege and terror of being a prophet was no longer restricted just to a few; all would hear the word of the Lord through the power of the Spirit. Joel 2 paints the picture of the day of the Lord in two panels. First, there are those who have reason to be terrified by the closeness of God but, even as the inexorable armies of God approach, there is still God's offer of forgiveness. The Lord exhorts, 'Rend your hearts and not your clothing' (Joel 2:13). The Lord desires to extend mercy; destruction is our choice, not God's; the Lord desires to be present with the people, offering the use of the great name, the Lord, as a shield and defence: 'everyone who calls on the name of the L ORD will be saved' (2:32). In this second panel, the Spirit is poured out on all so that they can see the gracious and saving nature of the Lord and respond.

This is the context of Pentecost and of Peter's quotation of Joel in Acts 2. The Lord has come close in Jesus Christ and offered, as the Lord always offers, the opportunity to repent and receive forgiveness marked by the gift of the Holy Spirit.

It is important to note this background to the way in which the Spirit speaks by the prophets. It is a sign of the closeness of God, a commissioning to speak of the decision to be made: rend our hearts and return to the Lord, or turn away? There is some evidence that the outpouring of prophecy on ordinary believers began to make people forget that the Holy Spirit's gifts are just that: gifts. They are not an ordinary human capacity, and they do not function under human control. They are divine gifts and serve the purpose that the Holy Spirit is always advancing: the building up of the body of Christ. In 1 Corinthians we are given an insight into a group of people very interested in the dramatic gifts of the Spirit, such as prophecy, which they seem to see as conferring or endorsing status in the Christian community. Paul has to keep reminding them that there is no such thing. No one is more important than any other and no one's gifts are earned or deserved. All are given for the benefit of the whole community.

'Strive for the greater gifts,' Paul implores (1 Corinthians 12:31) as he launches into his passionate description of the greatest gift of all: love. This is the gift the Corinthians – and we – should be seeking; this is the gift that prophecy serves, drawing people back to the grace and mercy of the love of God. This is 'inspiration' – the Holy Spirit, breathing the new life of God in us to draw us into relationship with the God who is love.

The excitement of being able to prophesy seems to have gone to the heads of some in the early church. For example, the group of Christians usually designated as 'Montanists' were accused of forgetting the proper distinction between the Holy Spirit and the human spirit. They are quoted as believing that the union between their great prophets and God was so deep that they could speak directly as God, not distinguishing as the prophets of old did between the word of the Lord and their own words. They are also claimed to have believed that the new prophecies they announced could add to or even supersede the Bible.[11]

Marcion's (circa 85–160 CE) views were very different from those of the Montanists but put forward a similar exercise of Christian freedom in relation to the Bible. Marcion argued that the god of the Old Testament is not the god encountered in Jesus Christ. Marcion lived and taught before most of the canon of the New Testament had been fixed, but it is clear that the New Testament does not lend itself to Marcion's interpretation. The New Testament frequently quotes the Old and refers to the way in which the coming of Christ fulfils the prophecies of the Old Testament. When 2 Timothy 3:16 says, 'All scripture is God-breathed,' it is referring as much to the work of the Spirit in the Old Testament as in the New, since these are the holy Scriptures that 'Timothy' would have learned in his infancy (2 Timothy 3:15). It is the same God who creates all things who also comes to renew all things. God is always Trinity, Father, Son and Holy Spirit, self-giving and self-receiving love. The thread of the purposeful, creative, self-giving love of God, Father, Son and Holy Spirit, runs through the whole of Scripture.

The Creed's affirmation of the way in which the Holy Spirit speaks through the prophets carries the weight of this history behind it. It is declaring a trust in the way God has been revealed to us, through the reading and hearing of the word of God, and issuing a reminder that God comes to us and speaks to us from outside ourselves and our own capacities. God comes to us as gift, which cannot be earned or instrumentalised but remains always as part of the presence of the Holy Spirit, building the body of Christ, calling and enabling witness to our filial calling. When the Creed calls the Holy Spirit the one who 'has spoken through the prophets', it is a reminder that God is not our creation. We have been given markers of the way in which God acts and speaks to enable us to bring our own action and speech to judgement. The Bible and the Church are among God's great, cleansing gifts because they eliminate the idols, the gods we make in our own image, and bring us back to the work of the Holy Spirit, the inspirer.

We believe in one holy catholic and apostolic Church

As a result of all that has been said about the Holy Spirit, the Creed goes on to declare that we can also 'believe' the Church to be the people in whom the work of the Spirit is ongoing, recreating the likeness of Christ in us, and so recreating the whole human race 'in the image of God'.

The way in which these clauses about the Church are stated in the English version of the Nicene Creed slightly blurs what is being said. In most early versions of the Creed in Latin and Greek, we declare that we believe 'in' the Father Almighty, the only begotten Son and the life-giving Spirit, but we 'believe' the Church.[12] The Church is to be trusted, not in its own right but because it is the work of the Spirit. This is perhaps particularly important in an age which acknowledges with pain and anger that the Church has not been worthy of trust in so many things. This clause in the Creed is not a blanket call to blind obedience in an institutional church but an acknowledgement of what the Church is and what it is not. It is not God. It does not speak with its own authority; it is wholly dependent on God.

But this clause does ask those who say the Creed to 'believe' that the Church is a gift of God, part of God's faithful, ongoing, creative and recreative work. Ephesians 1:4 says, 'He chose us in Christ before the foundation of the world to be holy and blameless before him in love.' This community of Christ's people is part of the original creating work of God, and its holiness and forgiveness is held 'in Christ', not in itself. It seems clear that this 'choosing' that Ephesians speaks of is not a process of choosing particular people throughout the history of the world, people who are already virtuous and ready for inclusion. It is a much grander scheme, comparable with God's whole work of creation from nothing. Everything is the gift of God. Just as God created multiplicity and abundance 'in the beginning', so 'in the fulness of time' God will gather up what God has made into Christ. Ephesians 1:8 speaks of this as the 'mystery' at the heart of the Church's life and calling: that it is a symbol of creation and the promise of fulfilment.

The Church's 'holiness', according to Ephesians, is 'lavished' on it through the forgiveness offered in the death of Christ. It is holy only as it receives forgiveness; it is holy only in its reception of the gift of alien righteousness, not demonstrated, not earned, but lavished on the Church to enable it to witness to the mercy and forgiveness of God, offered to all in Jesus Christ. Of this, the Holy Spirit is the 'pledge' (Ephesians 1:14). We believe in, we trust, the Holy Spirit at work in the Church.

Ephesians brings out the dynamic of what is being said about the Church – and what is not. The human institution of the Church, and all of its people, remains dependent day by day upon the forgiveness of God, Father, Son and Holy Spirit. Holiness is always borrowed, never our possession; the Church is holy only because it is forgiven, and because it seeks and offers forgiveness. The logic of the Lord's Prayer is evident, too, in this description. We only fully receive forgiveness as we forgive.

The 'Holy' Spirit is the means by which this costly, borrowed holiness is offered, in the life of the people of God. The work of discipleship is a work of receiving sanctification from the one whose nature it is: God. As people living day by day, in time, sanctification is a way of life, not a possession. It is freely given but needs to be renewed daily. Paul's great theological declarations about the work of God in Christ and the blessings offered to believers are nearly always followed by detailed advice and exhortation to live in what we are offered, not ever to take it for granted or to assume it is ours by right. Christians, the Church, the people of God, have to receive holiness every day as a matter of practice, not an abstract quality. Holiness can only be learned through receiving forgiveness and living together in love.

That is why the descriptions of the Church as one, holy and catholic all go together. In the purposes of God, the Church is the beginning of the new creation, a home for all who will respond to God's invitation and receive God's imparted holiness, won through the death of Christ and offered in the gift of the Spirit. There cannot be 'churches', plural, any more than there can be 'creations', plural. 'Churches' are a potent symbol of the innate lack of holiness that should drive us back to the merciful forgiveness of God. The New Testament's whole theology of the Church is about unity. Paul characterises the Christian community as 'the body of Christ' (Romans 12:3; Ephesians 4:16; 1 Corinthians 6, 12, 13 etc.): how can Christ have more than one body? We read in 1 John 1:28, and in the whole Johannine emphasis on unifying love as the demonstration of God, that we 'abide' in Christ together. And 1 Peter 2 reminds the Christian community that they were once disparate, 'not a people', but that they are now 'a chosen race, a royal priesthood, a holy nation, God's own people' (1 Peter 2:9). John the Seer glimpses the mighty battle of the end times, which results in 'a new heaven and a new earth' (Revelation 21:1). This is just as much the work of the Creator, now fully present with creation, at the heart of the great city which has no gates, and where all peoples and nations are at home.

The Holy Spirit in the Creed

Fundamental to the character of the Church is that it stands as a symbol of God, Creator, Redeemer, Fulfiller. There is only one holy God throughout all time and in all places. The Church is the sign of this God, and lives wholly dependent upon the action of Father, Son and Holy Spirit. The Church is a symbol of the 'catholicity' of God, One God who is always, everywhere, at all times.

In the period in which the Nicene Creed was formulated, the Church was no more united than it is today. In particular, the years of persecution before the conversion of the first Christian emperor of the Roman Empire in the fourth century led to huge splits among Christians. Those who responded to persecution with courage and a refusal to deny their faith often paid a terrible price for their confession of faith and, perhaps understandably, when persecution ebbed, felt that they had won the right to call themselves the true Church, the true holy ones, and to deny membership to the weaker Christians.

It is hard not to sympathise with this attitude, but the problem is that, as with current church divisions, it can lend itself to an apparent belief that holiness can ever be a human possession, and that the boundaries of the Church can ever be laid out by human beings. And this begins to break the theological logic of creation through to fulfilment, as though God the Creator is one kind of God, a bit profligate and with no very obvious purpose in creation; whereas God the Redeemer and Sanctifier is another kind of God, a bit more choosy, ruthless and interested only in some of creation. Salvation is in danger of becoming a human work, open only to those with the necessary qualities to receive what has been achieved by Christ's death.

The creedal declaration that we believe the Church to be one, holy and catholic says, instead, that the Church belongs in this declaration of dependence upon the work of God, Father, Son and Holy Spirit. God is the only reason why the Church is worth anything at all, let alone our trust and belief. If it is not one, holy and catholic, redeemed, restored and forgiven, then there is no point to it at all.

It is also the only reason why the Church is called to be 'apostolic'. The word's primary meaning is 'sent'. In the Creed, it neatly serves a double purpose. By association with its New Testament use – to describe the first apostles, who lived with Jesus and testified to all that they saw – it bases the Church's ongoing witness on that testimony. The Church is not at liberty to change the gospel it has received. We are called to 'proclaim afresh in each generation',[13] but we are not called to make afresh for each generation. The Declaration of Assent goes on to remind those making this declaration that witness is 'led by the Holy Spirit'. The apostolic witness of the Church belongs with the Spirit's work of 'speaking through the prophets' as well as with the Church's call to be one, holy and catholic. God is the same in every generation, and God's action for us is offered freely through Christ in the power of the Spirit in every time and place.

The first aspect of the Church's apostolic nature is this dependence upon what we have been given: the good news that the first apostles witnessed and handed on. The second is that each generation in turn is 'sent' to witness and hand on the good news. The Church does not exist for its own sake; it must not be complacent and inward-looking; its whole character as sign and symbol of the action of God demands that it offers the gift it has received: the gift of the Holy Spirit's testimony to Christ, the Son of the Father.

Augustine's description of the Holy Spirit as gift draws us into the whole gift-giving and receiving economy of God. Nothing is 'owned' by any one person within the Trinity; everything is shared; each person gives and receives themselves from the others, and all give themselves to what is made. So in the

Church, nothing is owned; all gifts are given to be shared. No one individual or group can be 'Church' without the others. All are sent to show and tell the world that it is beloved, that it is redeemed by God's gift of costly forgiveness, that the Holy Spirit gives new life in Christ to the glory of God the Father. This is what it means to say that the Church is 'one, holy, catholic and apostolic', not by nature but by grace, not by its own goodness but by the gift of the Holy Spirit.

We acknowledge one baptism for the forgiveness of sins

Baptism liturgies make reference to the work of the Holy Spirit, who, with the Father and the Son, brings us into new life in Christ. The Holy Spirit is also invoked over the water of baptism, as over the bread and wine in a Eucharistic service, to empower the ordinary things to be carriers of God's grace and life.[14]

The role of the Holy Spirit in baptism comes, in the first place, from the descent of the dove at the baptism of Jesus, as recounted by all the gospels. There is no suggestion that the Holy Spirit is absent from Jesus' life before his baptism – indeed, Luke tells us that it is through the Holy Spirit that Mary is able to bring Jesus, the Son of God, into the world at all (cf. Luke 1:35). But at his baptism, Jesus receives a full declaration of God's love, trust and approval for the mission he is to engage in through his life and into his death. Jesus' baptism assures Jesus that he is 'the beloved Son' (Matthew 3:17; Mark 1:11; Luke 3:22; John 1:32–34).

Christian baptism offers that same affirmation to those baptised: through the Holy Spirit, the baptised, too, become 'beloved children', sisters and brothers of the Son in the love of the Father. The relationship of the baptised to God is not a right but a gift, another symbol of the Spirit's gift-giving nature. In the provocative conversation that Jesus has with Nicodemus (John 3), Jesus explains to Nicodemus that the Spirit is free to bestow this gift outside the normal human guidelines that Nicodemus expects. Nicodemus has been born into the privilege of being one of the people of God, but he needs to let go of that as his anchor and to be born again, not of the flesh but of the Spirit (John 3:6). This picks up on the promise in John 1:12–13 – that the coming of Jesus is to invite all to become children of God. Our 'natural' birth and status is of no interest to God; it cannot bring us into the family likeness of the Son; only the gift of the Holy Spirit in baptism does this.

The same dynamic is at work in John the Baptist's fierce call to the baptism of repentance. It is not enough, John says, to rely on family faith, to say, 'We have Abraham as our ancestor' (cf. Luke 3:8); everyone needs to repent and start again.

Paul picks up the same themes in 1 Corinthians 12, reminding his hearers that 'in the one Spirit we were all baptised into one body', whether they were originally 'Jews or Greeks, slaves or free' (1 Corinthians 12:13). In the context of this passage, Paul is emphasising again that all the gifts of the Spirit are given to the whole body. No one is privileged by wealth, status, birth or the nature of the gifts they exercise; the Holy Spirit is the source of everything of value in the Christian community.

While the primary emphasis in baptism is on the free gift of love – the power the Holy Spirit gives to each to become children of God, siblings of the Son – there is also a sombre aspect to baptism. It involves letting go as well as receiving. Jesus is baptised as a mark of solidarity with the human race that he has come to save. In Matthew, John the Baptist vocalises the strangeness of baptising someone who has no sin (Matthew 3:13). Baptism is about repentance, and Jesus has nothing to repent for, unlike the rest of us.

The theme already outlined, about letting go of natural privilege in order to receive the baptismal gift of the Spirit, is brought into sharper focus by Paul in Romans 6:3–4. The language is not just about rebirth into the new but about the death of the old. Baptism, Paul says, is 'into death'; our old life is buried with Jesus; there is no other way of stepping from one life to the other; there is no pathway to new life that does not go through the death of the old life.

This theology of baptism came under pressure in the divisions in the Church during the period around the time when the Nicene Creed was being developed. Did Christians who had denied their baptism under persecution need to be rebaptised? The Creed comes down firmly on the side of what has become Christian orthodoxy: there is one baptism only. No one needs to be rebaptised. If baptism is the death of the old, then even if people turn back into the valley of the shadow, Sheol, the place of the dead, their death to the old life has taken place. Learning to live in the new life of Christ, the gift of the Spirit, might be a lifetime's work, but the first, unrepeatable death has happened.

The Creed's emphatic statement that 'we believe in one baptism' also works together with the other statements about the 'one holy catholic and apostolic Church'. The Spirit's gift of baptism incorporates people into the one body of Christ; it is a gift given in and through this body, not bestowed by individual groups or denominations of Christians. Someone baptised in one part of the world is still baptised if they move to another, because the gift is not the possession of any local church but of the one, Spirit-endowed Church.

The desire to be rebaptised is understandable. Those who have been baptised as children might long to experience their baptism again as adults; those who have been baptised in one tradition might wonder if their baptism was valid, particularly if they then come to an exercise of their faith in a tradition that looks for overt signs of baptism in the Spirit, such as speaking in tongues. But the theology of the Creed would suggest that the overt sign of baptism is a commitment to the unity of the body of Christ. The Holy Spirit enables death and rebirth into this community, bought with the death of Christ.

The Creed also says that baptism is 'for the forgiveness of sins'. This, too, is part of the same argument about the death of one life and the rebirth into another. 'Sins' are not just naughty things that individuals do but symptoms of a world in ignorance of or in rebellion against its Creator. This is the world that 'dies' in baptism, as the baptised person is reborn into the new life in Christ, which is the life of the renewed humanity, the 'beloved' children of God, in whom the Holy Spirit prays the words of the Son, 'Abba, Father'. Baptism is a renunciation of evil and a turning to Christ. Sins are clearly still committed by baptised Christians, but with confession and repentance they no longer bind us in solidarity with a disobedient world. Our baptismal forgiveness and ongoing need for forgiveness is not earned; it is a gift of the Spirit. Like any gift, it needs to be used, not neglected.

Baptism, particularly in older rites, has in it elements of cleansing and casting out the devil, which indicate that what is going on is exactly that work of the Spirit that has been detailed. What is happening is a death and rebirth, a liberation from the stranglehold of a world in rebellion against God. Baptism can be described as a form of exorcism – casting out the evil one, who has no lasting hold on a child of God reborn in the Spirit.

The theology of the Creed echoes the theology of the Lord's Prayer in this, too. The baptised are entering the kingdom, where the name of God is hallowed by forgiven and forgiving people, brought into the body of Christ, the Son's response to the Father, in the Spirit. As Jesus ascends to the Father in Matthew 28:19, this is the good news that is gifted to the disciples to enable them to demonstrate the authority that has been given to Jesus: the disciples are commissioned to 'make disciples of all nations, baptising them in the name of the Father and of the Son and of the Holy Spirit'.

We look for the resurrection of the dead, and the life of the world to come

The final clause of the Creed comes full circle. God, who created all things in the beginning, brings them to fulfilment in the 'world to come'.

What is being said here is that because of what we believe about God, we also believe that created life is not a temporary project for God but one to which God is faithful and committed, sharing God's own life with what God has made.

Life beyond death is not innate to human beings; the biblical view is not of a pre-existent soul which enters the body at some point and can leave it when the body dies. Instead, the Bible looks for a 'new creation', whose reality is intimately, though mysteriously, connected to the current creation through the presence and action of God.[15]

The incarnation of the Son and the ongoing presence of the Spirit are promises of weight: they demonstrate the worth God gives to creation. Creation is capable of receiving God's self-gift, though never of owning it as a possession. The Creed is able to declare faith in the 'resurrection of the dead' only because it has already been seen in the resurrection of the Son.

In Jesus' own mission, he reportedly raised at least two people from the dead – Lazarus and the son of the widow of Nain. But these two men were restored to a life in which, at the proper time, they would die again. Only Jesus himself was raised into 'the life of the world to come'. This was not a miracle. It was not something that happened within the created world, however unusual; instead this was the action of God's eternal life breaking into created reality from 'outside', from the 'place and time' of God, which is why creation, resurrection and new creation belong together: none of them is imaginable without the God in whom the Creed invites trust.

In 1 Corinthians 15, Paul makes it clear that the resurrection of Jesus is part of the earliest witness of the Christian community, and that it was no easier to believe in the first century than it is now because there were no precedents. But Paul argues that 'if Christ has not been raised, your faith is futile and you are still in your sins' (1 Corinthians 15:17). It is not incidental to Christian faith whether or not Jesus is raised from the dead because it is part of what is claimed about the character of God, and the reason for trust in God's faithfulness. Paul's hearers are obviously facing the same kind of questions that arise every time the 'place and time' of God are pictured: human reasoning can only function within created space and time. They want to know 'what kind of body' the resurrection body is (15:35), and, in response, Paul draws their attention to the original creative work of God, who makes all the kinds of bodily life that we take for granted, including the 'glorious' life of the sun, moon and stars (15:41). The God who can do this, fitting every kind of creature to its appropriate physical being, can be trusted to bring a resurrection body into being, too, even though it is not yet imaginable within the confines of current human experience, except as it is seen in Christ.

The trust in the resurrection of the dead as part of trust in God belongs in this section of the Creed because it is part of the good news to which the Church witnesses, and because it, too, is associated with the work of the Holy Spirit. Romans 8:11 assures its hearers that 'the Spirit of him who raised Jesus from the dead dwells in you'. The life-giving Spirit is already at work in the Christian community, enabling the death and rebirth of baptism, offering the foretaste and downpayment of the life of the world to come (Ephesians 1:13–14).

The life of the world to come is also part of what the community of Christ, the Church, is preparing for. The Creed speaks of a 'world' to come, paralleling the world 'in the beginning'. The resurrection of the dead is to a life shared, rather than just a promise to disparate individuals. Jesus' promises about the coming world are all about a new community, the kingdom, a whole new realm. In it, banquets are spread for the motley crew whom God invites; mansions beyond number are prepared for the weary who long for home; the people of the Beatitudes, of no apparent significance now, will be citizens of this world alongside forgiven thieves and any number of others whom God has invited. The Church is a sign and a foretaste of this community, preparing all for a world that can reflect the character of God, Father, Son and Holy Spirit, where personhood is a gift of self to and from the other, an invitation into a spacious and dynamic unity.

The hope of the life of the world to come does not lead to quietism or an acceptance of the broken and damaging reality of this world in the assurance that it will all be over soon. It is not 'the opium of the people' but a challenge to a gloomy acceptance of the status quo. The hope of the resurrection and the life of the world to come draws the people of the Creed into spiritual warfare against the principalities and powers that try to convince human beings that this realm is theirs. Just as the crucifixion of Christ exposes and judges human judgements, so the resurrection of Christ challenges human foreclosures. The Gospels reveal the complicity of all in the crucifixion: Jesus' friends, the ordinary people of the city, the religious authorities and the state authorities all judge that Jesus must die. But the verdict of God says otherwise, as God raises Jesus from the dead. The eternal life of God now wears the face of Jesus, whom *we* crucified.

The Spirit that raises Jesus from the dead is also, therefore, a Spirit of judgement on all human attempts to shut down the future of God's coming, whether through fear, despair, hatred or arrogant assumptions about power. None can withstand the judgement of the One who raised Jesus from the dead and can never be defeated.

The Creed says that, from beginning to end, the world is God's and only God can tell it its meaning and purpose. So many myths and narratives tell the world that it is doomed and dying because its life and its meaning are exhausted. But the Creed says that life and meaning do not rest with creation but with the Creator. The acts and the gifts of the Holy Spirit are the assurance that God is as God is shown in the life, death, resurrection and ascension of Jesus Christ. God is for us. The Holy Spirit holds open all the bridges between this world and the life of the world to come, and this is what 'we believe'.

Questions for further thought

1 Is it a new idea that the Creed says that Son and Spirit are also 'creators'?
2 Do you usually direct your prayer to Father, Son or Holy Spirit, or to 'God'?
3 Above, it is suggested that worship glorifies God – that is, it makes us aware of the presence of God. What do *you* think 'worship' is?
4 Why does what the Creed says about the Church belong with what it says about the Holy Spirit?

6
The Holy Spirit, the Giver of Life

The Holy Spirit is our connection to God. God acts decisively for us and for our salvation as the Son becomes human to live and die with us. The Spirit, the Giver of Life, raises Jesus from the dead into the life of the world to come. But the Holy Spirit ensures that the life of Jesus, God's action for us, remains part of every history, not just 'once upon a time' but always.

The Holy Spirit, who speaks through the prophets, draws every Christian community and every disciple of Christ into the story God tells the world of its meaning and purpose. The Holy Spirit connects God-for-us with God in God's transcendent eternity. This is what enables our witness to be truthful, if never complete, because there is a genuine connection with God in God's own reality and God as we come to know God in action for us and with us. This chapter will trace the way in which we can follow the thread of the Holy Spirit's work between us and God, which enables us to say, with trust and hope, 'We believe.'

Immanent/economic: reading back into God

The Christian understanding of God as Father, Son and Holy Spirit cannot be deduced. God can only be known in this way because God chooses to be known. This is what is meant by 'revelation'. While some might find this frustrating, with its corollary that God cannot be proved to exist, it is actually characteristic of God as the Creed describes God. The Creed says that God is the 'Father Almighty, maker of heaven and earth'. Everything that exists is part of the creative work of God, but God is not made; God creates the world in a way that gives it genuine separation and so genuine freedom in relation to God.

Two things follow on from this: the first has already been mentioned, which is that God cannot be read from creation. There is no necessary, ontological connection between God and creation: creation is not part of God's being; God is not incomplete without creation. Of course, creation inspires awe, wonder, fear, reverence; it is numinous in its power and beauty. The psalmist describes this as 'the heavens . . . telling the glory of God' (Psalm 19:1). But the same psalm goes on to say that human beings are given something more, something that 'tells the glory of God' not just by shouting out the presence of divinity but by describing God's character. The heavens speak of 'God', but the Law speaks of the 'Lord', the one who has reached out to Israel and called them into relationship.

This is the second thing that follows on from the freedom given to creation by God. God invites human beings not into the mindless obedience of servitude but into relationship, freely offered, freely received. God tells God's own holy Name and names each individual, counts every hair on their head (Luke 12:7); Jesus calls his followers not servants but friends (John 15:15).

The Creed makes it clear that revelation of the eternal character of God flows into time from the shattering event of the incarnation, the Son's entry into history, into humanity, into time, into death. But it also insists that this is not a new God who is being revealed in Christ but the 'maker of heaven and earth'. What God shows us about God in Christ is true of the eternal reality of God, even if our words and imaginations cannot entirely cope with the 'glory' that is revealed.

The Holy Spirit, the Giver of Life

The point of God's self-revelation is not so that theological speculation about God's divine reality can flourish but so that human lives can be invited into the Father's self-gift through Jesus Christ in the power of the Spirit. God's self-revelation is to enable us to live as sisters and brothers of the Son, filled with the Holy Spirit. Revelation is for our good, not for anything that God needs from us. Trinitarian theology needs to keep returning its gaze to the human community that is called into being by God, and the lives of individual disciples with and for that community. Arguing powerfully against the theological instinct towards abstraction rather than discipleship, Catherine Mowry LaCugna writes:

> The doctrine of the Trinity is ultimately therefore a teaching not about the abstract nature of God, nor about God in isolation from everything other than God, but a teaching about God's life with us and our life with each other.[1]

The challenge is a serious one to a human desire to ask abstract questions rather than life-changing ones. Theological discourse has sometimes been caricatured as asking how many angels could dance on the head of a pin. This debate probably never happened among scholastic philosophers, however much theologians like Aquinas and Duns Scotus loved unanswerable philosophical questions, but it pokes fun at exactly the abstraction that Mowry LaCugna warns against. The point of Christian faith is Christian life.

Mowry LaCugna also insists that God's self-revelation is not just a matter for individual faith but for 'our life with each other'. The Creed is making claims about the whole of reality, not just putting in a bid for individual spirituality or piety, important as those are. But the potential danger of an impatient dismissal of speculation about God's eternal reality in isolation from us is that God can be used to validate a way of 'life with each other' that a particular group or society deems ideal. For example, the argument could be made that society in the West has become too individualistic, leaving people isolated and lonely, and that a Trinitarian picture of God might encourage us to emphasise community and mutuality. A 'social' doctrine of the Trinity highlights the Threeness of God, three beings working in harmony and equality, acting as a challenge to our argumentative and hierarchical society. 'Let us be more like the Trinity in our lives together,' goes the argument, 'and human society will be a nicer place.'[2]

The problem with this approach is that it is in danger of instrumentalising God. God becomes an image of the kind of society human beings think we should want, and that image is likely to change from one generation to another, leaving the doctrine of God at the mercy of human self-understanding. It becomes less about God's gracious and saving self-revelation and more about humanity's anxious and partial self-discovery.

The theology that is summarised by the Creed does indeed suggest that human society and the character of God interact, but the emphasis is always on the proactive revelation of God rather than on the human capacity to know and shape the world. If Christian theology is not just human need and subjectivity in disguise, then 'revelation' is an essential concept, and what we come to know about God through revelation must also rest on God's own reality. What God gives in revelation is not just a sop, the best the human imagination can cope with, but God's own being and nature. God shows us what God is really like, in God's inner life, even if our words will always be insufficient to enable us to picture the being who is both Three and One without compromising either of those terms. If this is how God comes to us, what must God be like in God's own being? That question makes the vital connection which enables the Creed's declaration, 'We believe': we trust that this is true, and we will live accordingly. Theologians speak of the 'immanent' Trinity – God with God, beyond us and our history – and the 'economic' Trinity – God as we come to know God in God's presence and action with us in time. More helpfully, this distinction is described as the difference between the 'theological' Trinity and the 'evangelical' Trinity.[3] For the doctrine of the Trinity to be evangelical, to be good news worth sharing, it must be true, otherwise it is not saving news that God is like this. It also undermines everything we claim about the nature of God if God is not truthful in self-revelation. Instead, the Creed, in its reading of Scripture, says that it is good news that God is like this, Father, Son and Holy Spirit, beginning and end of all things, and that the incarnation is 'for us and for our salvation'.

The work of the Holy Spirit in the evangelical Trinity is to draw us constantly into that salvation that God, Father, Son and Holy Spirit have prepared for us, and to enable us to live in this truth by teaching us how to be children of God, sisters and brothers of the Son. The Holy Spirit forms the connection for us between the theological and the evangelical Trinity by keeping the fatherly nature of God visible in the constant representation of the incarnate Son, and by holding the Son's love of the Father in daily reality, in lives lived in faithfulness to the Son. The Father and the Son give us the Holy Spirit; the Holy Spirit gives us the Father and the Son. The beneficent circle of Trinitarian love means that no one person of the Trinity is to be found without the others, even if the Holy Spirit is our daily way into the life given us in the Son, the life of the Father's only Son, full of grace and truth (John 1:14).

In what follows, we will trace the way in which the work of the Holy Spirit enables us to see, not abstractly but as good news to be lived in, the connection between God in God's own being – the immanent, theological Trinity – and God-for-us – the economic, evangelical Trinity. We will do this not just because it is quite interesting but because our call to be people of the Spirit in daily life rests on the truth of what God shows us.

Starting with Jesus

1 Jesus and the Spirit in the evangelical/economic Trinity

The Christian confession that God is Father, Son and Holy Spirit comes about through attention to what is happening in Jesus Christ. Christology forces a re-reading of God's history with the world from beginning to end. As Christian theologians wrestled with the most truthful and faithful way to describe the startling presence of God and God's saving action in Jesus Christ, both the shocking newness and the strange continuity in the understanding of God became clearer and clearer. In the Old Testament, God constantly offers relationship with people, constantly gives them the means to form themselves around God's character, for their own flourishing. God is utterly transcendent, beyond human imagining and control, unlike the idols that human beings make for themselves, but God is also fiercely and faithfully present and self-giving. God binds God's life and the life of God's people together in a covenant that asks far more of God than it does of the people. God promises to be available to people in the Law, in the Temple and in the words of the prophets. It is wholly unexpected that God should come to live directly with the people, a fully human life that is also fully the presence and action of God: unexpected but not illogical. The incarnation is astounding but also characteristic.

The inevitable and necessary focus on Jesus Christ, the Son of God, and on his relationship with the one he calls 'Father'

The Holy Spirit, the Giver of Life

can and frequently does obscure the role of the Holy Spirit in God's presence with us. Yet, as we have seen, in exploring the theology of the Cappadocians and Augustine in relation to the Holy Spirit, the narrative of Scripture does not make sense if the Holy Spirit is removed.[4] The Holy Spirit is vital to the New Testament's understanding of how the Son comes to live with us as Jesus and how continuing filial lives respond.

While the role of the Holy Spirit might be obvious after the resurrection and ascension of Christ, particularly in relation to Pentecost and to the charismatic gifts of the Spirit, these all follow, in the theology of the New Testament, from the Spirit's primary role as the Jesus-maker, the Son-giver.

Matthew and Luke both attribute the incarnation to the work of the Spirit. It is the Spirit who enables Mary to conceive the child, Emmanuel, God with us. Matthew says that Mary 'was found to be with child from the Holy Spirit' (Matthew 1:18) and goes on to describe Joseph's dream, with its foundation in the prophet Isaiah speaking of the young woman who will bear a son. The Holy Spirit who has spoken through the prophets, as the Creed says, emphasises this in Joseph's dream, so that Joseph will know that he is part of the overarching pattern of God's work.

In Luke, the angel reassures Mary about the practicalities of how she, an unmarried young woman, will have a child. The angel says, 'The Holy Spirit will come upon you, and the power of the Most High will overshadow you' (Luke 1:35).

An important point is being made here: Jesus is born 'not of blood or the will of the flesh or of the will of man, but of God' (John 1:13). Jesus' conception and birth are outside the normal processes at least to this extent: he stands outside the usual family ties, the things inherited from 'the seed' of his forefathers. Although the Gospels are also witnessing that Jesus is not born through the sexual act, they are more interested in the freedom this gives the child from the whole web of family ties, with the status and demands associated with them. Jesus is born by the Holy Spirit. There is also the immense gift of freedom and respect given to Mary, as Jesus' mother, in this process. She chooses to say yes to God and does not have to become the possession of a husband, handed over to him by her father, for this to be the case. Her Magnificat is the joyful song of a free woman on whom God has looked with favour (Luke 1:48).[5]

The Holy Spirit is next visibly present at Jesus' baptism. All four gospels recount this moment of Trinitarian revelation (Matthew 3:16-17; Mark 1:10-11; Luke 3:21-22; John 1:32-34). In John's Gospel, the testimony comes from John the Baptist, but it contains explicit reference to the presence of the Holy Spirit and the confirmation of Jesus as the Son of God.[6] This is the start of Jesus' public ministry, the first recognition, since Mary and Elizabeth rejoiced together, of who he is and what he has come for.

Jesus' baptism is a pivotal moment in the Gospels. The layers of symbolism are thick and overlapping in this one simple act. Among the many things that are going on here, first of all Jesus is anointed as Messiah and King through the descent of the Holy Spirit and the voice of the Father. Next, he willingly shoulders solidarity with the human race that needs to be baptised to cleanse it from sin, though he himself has no need of such cleansing. He steps down into the deep and turgid waters, which symbolise the watery chaos from which God draws all life 'in the beginning', the waters that are both the source of life and the symbol of death.[7] Here at his baptism, the adult Jesus receives again from the Spirit the mission that he was given at birth. Jesus freely accepts the baptism that signifies that he, the Son, will be obedient in all things, even death, to the Father, whom he glorifies, making the Father present and visible through his own life in the Spirit.

The Holy Spirit, the Giver of Life

In all the gospels, John the Baptist fulfils his own vocation as the forerunner when he anoints Jesus in baptism. John is Samuel to Jesus' David (1 Samuel 16:13), but whereas the Spirit of the Lord comes upon David at his anointing, Jesus is already full of the Spirit, as John explicitly declares. Jesus is the one who will baptise others in the Spirit. Jesus is both the gift of the Spirit and the giver of the Spirit.

The first three gospels then narrate that after this public confirmation of Jesus' ministry and his acceptance of it, the next, strange, act of the Holy Spirit is to drive Jesus into the wilderness to be tempted. Jesus' full identification with humanity is not just grafted on but fully received and lived into by Jesus. Like any human being from Adam and Eve onwards, Jesus is tempted to 'exploit' his relationship with God. Philippians 2:6–11 is a hymn that is almost a summary of what Jesus achieves in the temptation in the wilderness. Adam and Eve are tempted by the serpent with the picture of themselves as 'like God' (Genesis 3:4). Although God has already freely made them in God's image (1:27), giving them the likeness the serpent tempts them with, they seem to want to snatch it for themselves, as though they cannot be sure of it if it is gift but only if it is something they have grabbed for themselves. In the wilderness, Jesus steadfastly refuses to be tempted by the devil to define his own relationship with God, to make his own mark upon it. Instead, over and over again, he replies with the Spirit-inspired words of Scripture: 'One does not live by bread alone, but by every word that comes from the mouth of God' (Matthew 4:4); 'Do not put the Lord your God to the test' (4:7); 'Worship the Lord your God and serve only him' (4:10). Jesus receives his sonship, his likeness to the Father, as gift, not possession, as he speaks the Spirit's scriptural words of obedience and trust.

The Spirit continues to be a necessary part of the narrative of Jesus, the Son, throughout his ministry. When he returns from the wilderness temptations, he stands in his home synagogue and sets out his mission, again given in words from Isaiah, which announce the mission as enabled by the Spirit's presence and anointing (Luke 4:18–19). The Spirit is co-agent with Jesus, too, in his acts of power throughout his ministry. John's Gospel calls these miracles 'signs': they are not performed to draw attention to Jesus himself and his own powers but to highlight the presence of God and the coming of God's kingdom. They are performed as part of the commissioning that Jesus announces in Luke 4, the Spirit's announcement of the liberating power of the Lord's favour, rejoiced in by Mary, longed for by the poor, the captive, the oppressed.

Striking among these acts of power is Jesus' direct confrontation with evil in the form of what the gospels describe as demonic possession. In Matthew 12:28, Jesus says, 'It is by the Spirit of God that I cast out demons,' but it could be argued that all the works of power that Jesus performs come under this heading of fulfilling the Spirit's anointing of Jesus. Luke, in particular, also associates the Spirit with Jesus' practice and teaching on prayer, as seen in chapter 11. The chapter starts with Jesus himself at prayer and his disciples' request to be taught how to pray, in response to which Jesus teaches them the Lord's Prayer. The instruction that follows is not straightforward, but it focuses on learning through prayer to trust in the goodness of the Father's good gift of the Spirit (Luke 11:13). The theological connection with Paul's teaching on the Spirit's role in prayer is striking: it is the Spirit who enables believers to say the words that Jesus gives in the Lord's Prayer and to call God 'Abba, Father' as Jesus does (Romans 8:15–16).[8]

The Gospels give significant space to the narration of the death of Jesus and all that leads up to it. They do not attempt to hide the painful and shameful death that Jesus undergoes,

The Holy Spirit, the Giver of Life

but instead they concentrate on it. They show how, contrary to what might be expected, this does not suggest that Jesus' mission is a failure but instead confirms the saving work that the incarnation and death of Jesus achieves. Here, too, the Holy Spirit is closely associated with enabling the interpretation of Jesus' death. The fullest exposition of this is in John's Gospel, as Jesus prays for and instructs his disciples about his coming death in John 14–17. The Holy Spirit will teach the disciples how to understand Jesus' death as an act of obedience to the Father, rather than as the triumph of the 'ruler of this world' (John 14:25–35). The 'Spirit of Truth' will glorify Jesus as he enables the disciples to bear the truth (16:12–15). The Advocate will judge the false judgements that people have made about Jesus and his death (16:7–11). All of this clearly expects that the Holy Spirit is fully present with Jesus throughout the ordeal to come and is seen by Jesus as the interpreter for his disciples of his death. Again, in one of those strange theological continuities of thought, Paul's teaching in Romans 8 picks up this theme in relation to our own fear of death. The Spirit who gives us life is the Spirit who was with Jesus in death and who raised him again, and so is our hope and confidence as we live and die in 'the flesh' (Romans 8:9–11).

The connection between the Holy Spirit and the death of Christ is also highlighted in Hebrews. Hebrews has a long and complex discussion about the new and the old covenants between the people and the Lord and the role of the high priest in this covenant in offering sacrifices for sin. The author of this letter says that the Holy Spirit 'indicates that the way into the sanctuary has not yet been disclosed' in the Old Testament covenant and its practices for dealing with sin (Hebrews 9:8). It is not until the death of Christ, 'who through the eternal Spirit offered himself without blemish to God' (9:14), that the way to the sanctuary, the way to forgiveness of sin, is finally and fully opened (9:24–28). Jesus offers his death to the Father, for our sake, through the Spirit.

Paul explicitly associates the Holy Spirit with the resurrection of Jesus in the passage already discussed: 'The Spirit of him who raised Jesus from the dead' (Romans 8:11) and which influences the Creed's designation of the Holy Spirit as life-giver. But in Matthew, the risen Jesus instructs his disciples to baptise new believers in the threefold name (Matthew 28:19); in Luke, Jesus tells the disciples to wait until 'what my Father promised' comes upon them with 'power from on high' (Luke 24:49), which is picked up in the Acts narrative of Pentecost; in John, the risen Jesus breathes on the disciples and says, 'Receive the Holy Spirit' (John 20:22). In resurrection, as in conception, commissioning, ministry and death, the Holy Spirit is fully present and active in the incarnate life of Jesus.

Although the direct link between the risen Jesus and the witness and presence of the Spirit sounds almost like a reunion, a regaining of the full Oneness of the Spirit and the Son in the Godhead, it is nevertheless clear throughout the New Testament that the Son and the Spirit are not identical, even though they cannot be separated. The Holy Spirit is not an innate power but a personal presence that enables the Son to remain Son, even in the human life he lives and dies.

2 Jesus and the Spirit in the theological/ immanent Trinity[9]

Considerable caution is necessary in 'reading back' from how we encounter the work of the Holy Spirit in the incarnate life of the Son and human responses to it. But it has been argued above that there is a necessary connection between economic and immanent understandings of the Trinity. If God is not really like this in God's very being, then what is experienced of God is always unreliably mediated, leading to a degree of uncertainty,

The Holy Spirit, the Giver of Life

at the very least, about the truth claims being made. The Creed makes a claim on those who recite it, to testify that the world is like this because God is God who is Father, Son and Holy Spirit in God's very being, not just as we imagine God. With careful humility about the limits of human comprehension of the divine, nonetheless, 'we believe' that God chooses to show us God truly.

This suggests that the pattern of action and, in particular, the pattern of relating that is discernible in God's interaction with created beings gives us deep clues about the reality of God, not so that we can play the detective in relation to God but so that we can continue to trust the truthfulness of God's saving work with us.

The New Testament witnesses to the action of the Holy Spirit in bringing the Son of God to human birth and in confirming that sonship in human form, in Jesus' baptism, in the temptation in the wilderness and in Jesus' mission and ministry. All that Jesus is and does is in the power of the Spirit and to glorify the Father.

This might provide some insight into the dilemma of the 'origins' of the Son and the Spirit in relation to each other and to the Father. The two classic approaches are either that the Father is the 'source' of the Son and the Spirit, or that the Father and the Son together are the source of the Spirit. But the biblical witness suggests another and possibly less divisive account: it is the Holy Spirit who is the source of the Son and so of the fatherly reality of the Father. In the incarnation, the Holy Spirit brings the Son to birth in Mary. The very fact that he is 'the Son' already presupposes the full participation of the Father in this. On this account, then, it is the Father and the Spirit who are the source of the Son. The Son and the Spirit present – glorify and make present – the Father's love. Thus, the Son and the Spirit are the source of the Father. The Son is the love of God made visible so that all are invited to participate in the Son's love of the Father through the Spirit. In that case, the Son is the source of the Father and the Spirit. Reading back from the Bible seems to suggest a much more perichoretic understanding of the relations of origin than the classic disagreement would suggest. No person of the Trinity is possible without the others. Each presents and glorifies the others. Reading back from the New Testament witness, the eternal being of God is the circling dance without beginning or hierarchy, where every possible answer about who comes first, Father, Son or Holy Spirit, is the right answer.

It is more difficult – and more controversial – to read back from the crucifixion into the reality of the eternal life of God, and that is, perhaps, because those who attempt it generally do not give a role to the Holy Spirit in this. But the Holy Spirit is the 'exegete' for us, the great teacher of the ways of God revealed in the Son, and therefore any account of the nature of God that leaves out the Holy Spirit needs to be questioned.

Some theologians from the second century onwards seem to have suggested that Jesus' suffering must also be the suffering of God.[10] The most easily dismissed version of this simply does not see genuine differentiation between the persons of the Trinity and so assumes that what we experience as three 'persons' is just God under different guises – in which case what the one we call Son suffers is the same as what the one we call Father suffers, since there is no real distinction between the two.

A much more nuanced and appealing account of how the cross reads back into the eternal divine life has been put forward over the last century or so. The argument rests on several compelling grounds, such as the scriptural witness to the passionate God, who cares about his people, is hurt by them and angry with them, and so is not unable to suffer. Added to this is a definition of divine love based on the human experience of love: love is costly and painful. If God does not suffer in loving us, then God does not genuinely love. Some of the most persuasive modern accounts also come from a Trinitarian theology that strongly emphasises the Threeness of God as opposed to God's Oneness. The Father suffers the loss of the Son, while the Son suffers the cross.[11]

There are a number of questions, however, about this approach. It discards the careful work done over the centuries about the limits of human language in relation to God and assumes that human experience is the best description of what it is to be God. We cannot love without suffering, so that must be true of God, too. Strangely, this approach gives little value to the genuine humanity of Jesus, simply assuming that his humanity is subsumed in the divinity of the Son: what Jesus suffers, God suffers. But it also demonstrates the weakness of the human imagination in relation to the Trinity: we think that we know what a father–son relationship is, and our focus is on what seems like a graspable interaction, which leaves the Holy Spirit on one side.[12] The suffering of Jesus on the cross becomes a kind of divine soap opera between Father and Son, not unlike the kind of interactions of the Greek pantheon. This dangerously undermines the Creed's declaration of God as 'maker of heaven and earth, of all that is, seen and unseen', because it assumes a simple continuum between God and creation, rather than an absolute difference between God and all that God has made.

God, the Creator of all things, does not need to become human in order to 'feel' what it is like. God is the life of all life; all things are held in being by God and are known and loved in a way that they do not know and love themselves. Jesus suffers terrible abuse, torture and brutal death, but he does not experience every kind of suffering known to humankind. If God does not 'understand' or 'feel' except what God experiences in Jesus, then God is still ignorant of most human experience. Instead, the truth is that God has God's own way of presence and action in what God has made. Always, in all times, the Holy Spirit has been witnessing to the love and self-giving of the Holy Trinity and drawing people into the filial response to that love. The Son does not become human in order to add anything to God but in order to save humanity through uniting it with the divine action. God becomes human so that we may learn how to be human in relation to God and to one another, set free to be in the image of the Son, in the power of the Holy Spirit.

Reading back from the cross into the divine reality of God's life does not mandate us to say that God suffers as we do, but it does enable us to believe and trust that, as Paul says, nothing 'will be able to separate us from the love of God in Christ Jesus our Lord' (Romans 8:39). Even suffering and death do not break the power of the Holy Spirit, the life-giver.

The gifts of the Spirit

1 The gifts of the Spirit to the world: the evangelical/economic gifts of the Spirit

One of Augustine's definitions of the Holy Spirit is that of 'gift'. The two interconnected, foundational gifts that the Creed ascribes to the Holy Spirit are life and new life. The Holy Spirit, with the Father and the Son, brings creation into being and gives it life, as only God can, because only God is alive with God's own life: everything else is made; it comes into being and it passes away; only God is eternal life.

We have already discussed the life-giving role of the Spirit, or Breath, of God in Genesis 2 and in Ezekiel's vision of the dry bones. In Genesis, God makes an image, the earthling, and breathes life into it: a Trinitarian picture of the full participation of all the persons of the Trinity in creation, as the Father forms human beings in the image of the Son, and the Spirit gives life.

The Holy Spirit, the Giver of Life

Other places in the Old Testament refer to the creative, life-giving work of the Spirit.[13] Psalm 104 is a lyrical description of the greatness of the Lord as demonstrated by creation in its beauty and abundance but also in its total dependence on the Lord:

> When you hide your face, they are dismayed;
> > when you take away their breath, they die
> > and return to their dust.
> When you send forth your Spirit, they are created;
> > and you renew the face of the ground.
>
> (Psalm 104:29–30)

Isaiah, too, looks to the creative work of the Spirit both as a challenge to human arrogance and as a source of hope and trust in God. The Lord's Spirit does not need human advice (Isaiah 40:13) and 'the everlasting God, the Creator of the ends of the earth. He does not faint or grow weary' (40:28).

The New Testament connects the life-giving work of the Spirit in creation with the hope and promise of new life in Christ. The Holy Spirit who brought the Son into the world through Mary also raises Jesus from the dead. These two ideas are theologically connected: they demonstrate the untrammelled life-giving power of the Spirit. In John 3, Jesus challenges Nicodemus to see the freedom of the Spirit, whose life-giving power is not limited by what human beings think is possible. 'How can anyone be born after having grown old?' Nicodemus asks (John 3:4), and Jesus replies, 'The wind blows where it chooses' (3:8); new birth in the Spirit is possible.

This promise forms the basis of what the New Testament says about the promise of new life for disciples of Christ, both the once-for-all rejection of the old life, signified by conversion and baptism, and the daily renewal of Christ-shaped life by the

Spirit, which is often called sanctification. Both of these are freely given gifts of the Spirit, not achievements of the believer. They come to us from outside our own possibilities, as gift, even though, like gift, they are not forced upon us.

Romans 8 makes precisely the same set of theological connections. The Holy Spirit 'who raised Jesus from the dead' now lives in believers: the source of all life now makes a home in the frailty of ephemeral human life and becomes the source of hope and renewal (Romans 8:9–11). The life-giving Spirit is intimately connected to Christ and the Christ-shaped life in the believer. Just as the Spirit gives earthly life and resurrection life to Christ, so, as the Spirit teaches believers how to be the children of God and siblings of the Son, human life is also reconnected to that divine circle of the life-giving love of Father, Son and Holy Spirit. The characteristic shape of the Spirit's gifts becomes clearer in this exposition. The gifts of the Spirit to the Church are always glorifying Christ, always making the life of the Son manifest in the world. The same dynamic is at work in the great prayer of Ephesians 3:14–19. The Spirit's power enables the life of Christ in believers, who find their family bond as children of the Father. Again, the Christ-shaped response to the Father becomes a gift from the Spirit in the life of believers.

A significant aspect of the life-giving gift of the Spirit is its power to liberate. Paul talks about the psychological struggle to be the people that we long to be. 'I do not understand my own actions. For I do not do what I want, but I do the very thing I hate' (Romans 7:15). He describes a lack of choice that feels both personal – 'I do what I do not want to' – but also constrained from outside – 'sin dwells within me' (7:17). From Genesis 3 onwards, this is the wholly recognisable sense of responsibility for our failures, coupled with inability to choose differently. Adam and Eve freely choose to disobey God, but they are also tempted by the serpent. Paul freely chooses not to follow the good commands of the law, and yet he feels constrained by something beyond himself in his misdoings. This discussion in Romans 7 leads into the declaration in Romans 8:2, 'For the law of the Spirit of life in Christ Jesus has set you free'. Similarly, in Galatians 5:1, Paul says, 'For freedom Christ has set [you] free,' and goes on to say in verse 16, 'Live by the Spirit.' Living in the Spirit gives the Galatian disciples freedom to become the people they long to be.

The freedom of the life given by the Spirit is the freedom of the children of God as manifested in Jesus' ability and willingness to be obedient to the Father in all things. Jesus is not constrained to act as he does; he is free to be who he most fundamentally is, which is the Son of God, and that is the freedom that grows in those in whom the liberating life of the Spirit is growing.

Writing in the fourth century, Athanasius explains that the Son becomes incarnate to restore in humanity the 'image' in which they were originally created: the Son-shaped image of the Father's love. Athanasius uses the metaphor of a portrait on wood that has become so dirty and stained that it is no longer recognisable, and can only be restored if the original sitter comes and enables the image to be redrawn.[14] Athanasius describes the sorry state to which humanity has descended, unable to do good, bound by sin and death until Christ undoes death's hold by his own death and offers himself as a sacrifice to redeem human beings from slavery to sin and to set them free to live and worship as they long to.[15]

The New Testament gives us examples of what this freedom looks like, not just in Jesus but also in some of his followers. Mary freely consents to cooperate with God and to bring the Son into the world, and her response is the hymn of praise that we call the Magnificat. In her freedom, she is able to glorify God: to see and name, with delight, the character of God. Paul, struck blind on the Damascus road, accepts the offer of freedom given by the one he has been persecuting, and at once 'he began to proclaim Jesus in the synagogues' (Acts 9:20). Peter, who was too frightened to acknowledge Jesus on the night before the crucifixion, teaches his people to 'believe in him and rejoice with an indescribable and glorious joy' (1 Peter 1:8). Peter and Paul are freed to acknowledge their former slavery and their inability to be the people they longed to be. They are set free to repent, and so to praise.

There is a striking dynamic of grace at work here that mirrors and counters the dynamic of sin. Just as sin is experienced both as an inward choice and as a lack of choice, so grace is experienced both as a choice made by the believer and as a gift from beyond. Where sin constrained, grace sets free.

2 The gifts of the Spirit in the theological/immanent Trinity

It is harder and even more speculative to read back the gift-giving nature of the Holy Spirit into the theological Trinity. But what is revealed in the notion of the Holy Spirit as gift is something fundamental to the character of God. God is God in total freedom. Nothing but God dictates the character of God. God's whole being, then, is gift, not requirement or constraint.

Unlike created beings, God does not require the gift of life, since God is life. The Name that God reveals to Moses is often translated as 'I AM', so fundamental is it to what God reveals of the divine being: it is dynamic and alive. On several occasions, mostly in John's Gospel, Jesus takes that great 'I AM' to define himself and his mission. In John's Gospel, the 'I AM' connects with Jesus as the one who brings life, freedom and salvation: 'I am the bread of life' (John 6:35); 'I am the light of the world' (8:12); 'I am the gate' (10:7) through which the sheep may enter into safety and freedom; 'I am the Good Shepherd' (10:11); 'I am

The Holy Spirit, the Giver of Life

the resurrection and the life' (11:25); and 'I am the true vine' (15:1).

In Mark 14:62, Jesus responds to the high priest's question about whether or not Jesus is the 'Messiah, the Son of the Blessed One' with the words 'I am'. The high priest recognises this as the claim that it is and labels it as blasphemy. It provides the perfect excuse the religious leaders have been looking for to condemn Jesus to death. The irony is understated but unmistakeable: how can the great 'I AM' die?

In all of these examples, Jesus is 'I AM' on behalf of others. His life is innately, unavoidably, generous. His 'I am' is not a claim to power that will save him but one that will save us. It is the mark of all God's activity towards us, flowing from the generosity of God's very being.

This generosity is seen in the way in which the three persons are 'given' to one another and by one another. The clumsiness of language cannot do justice to this idea, but it has to speak of the wholly 'unnecessary' character of Trinitarian divine being. It makes no sense to say that God 'chooses' to be Trinity, since this is who God is, and yet the idea is also insightful. God is not a static and solitary being but full of life, full of self-giving and self-receiving.

We have already suggested that a strong understanding of the Spirit enables a retelling of the 'origins' of Father, Son and Holy Spirit in relation to one another. The same kind of effect follows in naming the Holy Spirit as gift. It enables a way of seeing that the Holy Spirit in the eternal life of God might also be described as 'gift'. The Holy Spirit breathes the Son-shaped life of God in response to the Father-shaped life of God. The Holy Spirit gifts the Father's fatherhood and the Son's sonship[16] in a way that parallels how the Holy Spirit brings the Son to birth in history, enabling the Son to be glorified and made visible and so to glorify and make the Father visible. In turn, the Holy

Spirit receives the fatherliness of God, which 'brings forth' the Spirit, and the Son's self-gift as the one who makes the Father's fatherliness known. Each is a gift to the other. None is there just to work for the others. Each receives their being from the other two as gift, eternally.

The gifts of the Spirit in the world are about life and about new life, as children of God. That same gift has some echoes in the theological Trinity, in the generosity of God's life and in the openness of each to the other.

The gift of the Spirit in our experience is powerful but also self-effacing. What the Spirit gives is always the life of the Son of the Father, and the gifts that invite and enable human beings more and more to grow into the likeness of Christ. Although it is appropriate to see the whole being of God as gift-giving, the name of 'gift' is particularly appropriate for the Spirit as the one utterly given to the life of the Father and the Son.

Witness

1 The Spirit as witness in the evangelical/economic Trinity

One of the characteristics of the Spirit in the Creed is that the Spirit 'has spoken through the prophets'. In the Old Testament, prophetic speech is limited to those with a particular calling from the Lord to speak; in the New Testament, Peter declares that now the Holy Spirit is poured out on all people (Acts 2:17). What is 'poured out', in both cases, is the ability to testify to the work and the character of God. As with all the gifts of the Spirit, this calling to be witnesses comes from outside ourselves and our natural human capacities, and yet works within us, so that the action to which we draw attention becomes our own story, woven into God's story.

The repeated refrain in the Gospels is that the coming of Jesus 'fulfils' things that have been patterned into the witness of Scripture. For example, Matthew 1:22 says that the angel's message to Joseph is 'to fulfil what had been spoken by the Lord through the prophet', and in Matthew 2:17, the flight of Jesus' parents into Egypt fulfils a prophecy in Jeremiah. The crucifixion, too, has details that pick up the voice of the Holy Spirit, speaking in an earlier time but with resonance in Jesus' coming. In John 19:24, the venal soldiers dividing Jesus' possessions among themselves are unwittingly part of the pattern of witness, echoing Psalm 22:18.[17] After the resurrection, according to Luke's Gospel, Jesus meets some grief-stricken disciples on the road to Emmaus, and 'beginning with Moses and all the prophets, he interpreted to them the things about himself in all the scriptures' (Luke 24:27).

These regular Old Testament references in the Gospels serve to remind the reader and hearer that, though the birth, life and death of the Son of God came as a shock to those living through the time of the incarnation, nevertheless the incarnation was not a shock to God or something that was uncharacteristic. The words of prophecy, spoken with one set of meaning to their original hearers in the times of the Old Testament prophets, are reused in the Holy Spirit's care and witness in other times, too. The Holy Spirit, who speaks by the prophets, is not a time-bound creature. The Holy Spirit is God eternal and is able to weave together the threads that can only be seen sequentially in history but can be seen in eternity as one whole tapestry testifying to the loving action of God.

In particular, the New Testament use of these references makes it clear that the Holy Spirit's witness through Scripture, like all of the Holy Spirit's actions, is to glorify the Son, to bring the Son into view, for the glory of the Father. All of these references gather, like iron filings to a magnet, around the coming of the Son to live with us.

The witness of the Spirit to the Son is what continues to be poured out following the incarnation, so that the pattern of Scripture, focused around the Son, becomes clear to each generation, and so that each follower of Jesus Christ can pick up that witness and make it their own in word and deed.

The role of the Holy Spirit as witness and enabler of witness is perhaps particularly striking in John's Gospel and in Acts. In John 14:17, 14:26 and 16:13, Jesus calls the Holy Spirit 'the Spirit of truth', and in 16:8–11, he explains that the truth-telling of the Holy Spirit cuts through the false witness, the wrong judgements, of others about Jesus. This is a particularly poignant and important moment on the night before Jesus is about to be condemned to death by the perverse judges he will face. He warns the disciples that they, too, will face the wilful misjudgements of the people around them (John 15:18–25), but he says that the Spirit will 'testify on [his] behalf' (15:26). In Matthew's Gospel, the role of the Holy Spirit in enabling the disciples to understand and witness to Jesus even in persecution is also mentioned (Matthew 10:19). Only the Holy Spirit can enable Jesus' witnesses to see through the dark and apparently meaningless actions of history into the faithful action of God through it all.

In John, Jesus also calls the Holy Spirit a teacher (John 14:26). These two characteristics go together: the Holy Spirit teaches the world its truth, to be found in Jesus, and teaches Jesus' disciples how to live in that truth. Acts shows the early church living out the fearless witness that the Holy Spirit enables. From Pentecost onwards, the disciples speak and live as those who know Jesus and so know the shape of God's action. The first few chapters of Acts are particularly full of references to the Hebrew Scriptures (cf. Acts 2:17–21; 2:25–28; 2:34–35; 3:22–24; 4:11; 4:25–26). Stephen's long speech in Acts 7–8 is a precise living-out of what Jesus predicted: at this time of mortal danger, Stephen is enabled to witness to the pattern of God's action in Jesus Christ throughout the Scriptures. It is the Holy Spirit who sends Peter to Cornelius (10:19) and who directs Paul's missionary enterprises from the beginning, instructing the church in Antioch to set him apart for the work of the Spirit (13:2). A central part of Paul's missionary strategy wherever he goes is to explain how the Scriptures bear witness to Jesus and to the necessity of his suffering (for example, 17:3), enabling others to see the pattern of the Spirit's work of witness 'through the prophets'.

The witnessing work of the Holy Spirit through the Bible and in the testimony of the disciples is interconnected. The Bible gives confidence that what we are witnessing is the work of the never-failing faithfulness of God throughout time. As individuals tell this story again, their confidence and understanding deepens. It becomes a story of personal salvation as well as the work of God for the whole of creation. It becomes a story in which individual human beings are invited into the love between the Father and the Son through the witness of the Spirit of Truth.

The words are important: we live in the stories we tell about ourselves, and we make our choices and justify our actions according to that story. The Spirit of Truth witnesses in changed lives, not just in fine words.

Romans 8 is a particularly tightly argued theology of the Spirit, bearing witness to and enabling our changed reality. This chapter says that we live in the Spirit, are led by the Spirit and are liberated by the Spirit to enable us to become children of the Father, as the Son invites us to be. Our doubting and tremulous spirits require the witness of the Holy Spirit to give us courage to call upon the Father as siblings of the Son (Romans 8:16–17). The Holy Spirit stands beside us, giving us support, working with us, not instead of us.

The witness of the Spirit with our spirit enables hope in the face of the sufferings of the world because the Spirit draws us again into the overall picture, from creation to fulfilment, as in the Spirit's witness in Scripture. Praying in us and with us, in the meagreness and ignorance of our prayers, the Holy Spirit continues to witness to the unswerving faithfulness of God, even when all seems dark and meaningless. The Spirit as the enabler of prayer is a profound insight into why we are asked to pray: we pray for the coming of the kingdom, and as we do, we pray more and more as the ones who already live in that kingdom, and invite others, too.[18]

The Spirit's witness in changed lives of hope and trust is both personal and communal. The Spirit prays the Son's love of the Father in each individual who is becoming a child of God, but the Spirit also prays the Son's love of the Father in lives that are brought together to witness to the reality of the world made by the One God. In Galatians 5, Paul describes the patterns of living that destroy personal freedom and break communities apart. In contrast, he describes the 'fruit of the Spirit' (Galatians 5:22–26), which are all ways of behaving that prioritise others and build life together. This is sanctification. Holy lives are lives that build up the filial response of trust and the love of God in each person and enable others, too, to live in the holiness of life. This is the life lived in the Spirit and guided by the Spirit. This is the life that witnesses to Jesus Christ and to the invitation to human beings to become again the 'images' of God – in becoming daughters and sons, sisters and brothers, of the Son, through the Spirit.

2 The Spirit as witness in the theological/immanent Trinity

The Spirit's role as witness in the evangelical Trinity is the threefold cord of witness through Scripture, witness through testimony and witness in transformed lives. All of this is about witness to Jesus, to the Son-shaped calling that the Father offers

The Holy Spirit, the Giver of Life

through the Spirit. It is witness to the character of God as the Creed describes God.

Within the Godhead, there is no need for 'witness' of this kind. God is not in danger of forgetting God's character. And yet, as Augustine noted, the term 'Holy Spirit' does carry the character of the whole of God. God is holy, and God is spirit. God's holiness, which we are asked to mirror, is the holiness of self-giving and self-receiving love. God lives in the 'Spirit', not in the 'flesh' as Paul describes it: there is no selfishness in God, no self-serving or self-glorification among the persons of the Trinity. The 'life in the Spirit' that the Holy Spirit grows in the economy of God's action with us reflects the life in the Spirit in God's being.

In the economy, the Spirit is constantly at work to grow individual and corporate lives that witness to Jesus. In the immanent life of God, God's fatherliness gives the Second Person of the Trinity sonship in the Spirit. The Spirit brings forth the image of the Father, which is the Son, just as the Spirit in the economy remakes the image of the Son in us, so that we can pray to the Father. The Son 'witnesses' to the fatherliness of the Father, and the Father 'witnesses' to the Son as the one who is the Word and the image of the Father, so that even here, in God's eternal life, and even though the language is inadequate, something of the witnessing work of the Spirit, the Son-maker, has some meaning.

The good news that is carried by the relationship of the Son to the Father in the Spirit in the evangelical Trinity is based in this prior and eternal 'good news' of the character of God in God's own being. This is what is spoken over creation through the Word and Breath of God, 'the Father Almighty', whose fatherliness is given by the Spirit in the Son, and received by the Spirit through the Son, and responded to by the Son in the Spirit.

The Holy Spirit as the bond of love

1 The Holy Spirit as the bond of love in the evangelical/economic Trinity

In his earthly life, Jesus' commitment to his Father is at the centre of all that he does. Luke's Gospel shows us a vignette of Jesus as a child, irresistibly drawn to the Temple, the place where the Lord had promised to be found by his people. The child Jesus, quite unselfconsciously, calls it 'my Father's house' (Luke 2:49). In adult life, Jesus says that it is the purpose of his life to 'do the will of him who sent me', that is, the Father (John 6:38). Most movingly of all, in the garden of Gethsemane, Jesus acknowledges his own longing to avoid the cross but, even in this moment, prays, 'Not what I want, but what you want' (Mark 14:36). As Hebrews comments, this picture of Jesus makes it clear that the unity between Jesus and the Father is not automatic but chosen daily. 'Although he was a Son, he learned obedience through what he suffered' (Hebrews 5:8) and was 'tested as we are, yet without sin' (Hebrews 4:15).

In our own human experience, it is the Holy Spirit who prays 'Abba, Father' in us and grows us into the likeness of Christ the Son. Watching the earthly life of Christ, it seems that the shape of the work of the Spirit in the incarnate life of Christ is repeated in us. The Holy Spirit holds the Son in the love of the Father in his earthly life and, though we are not 'sons and daughters' in all eternity, as Christ is, the same kind of process is going on in us: we, too, are brought into the love between the Son and the Father through the Holy Spirit. The Holy Spirit takes up habitation in us, so that we become the Spirit's 'temple', where we, too, learn from the Father how to be children (cf. 1 Corinthians 6:19).

This function of the Holy Spirit as 'the bond of love' is visible from the beginning to the end of Jesus' life. It is the Holy Spirit

The Holy Spirit, the Giver of Life

who brings the Son of God to human birth and accompanies Jesus throughout his mission. And it is to the Holy Spirit that Jesus gives up his life on the cross, trusting that his life as the Son on earth is the Spirit's gift to the Father (Hebrews 9:14). This is the saving self-offering of the Son to the Father through the Spirit, who has prayed 'Abba, Father' in Jesus throughout his life and breathed the loving obedience of a Son in everything that Jesus did. On the cross, Jesus 'breathes his last' human breath, giving himself back to the Spirit, the life-giver (Matthew 27:50; Luke 23:46; John 19:30). There is something about this moment of death that makes a watching centurion say, 'Truly, this man was God's Son!' (Mark 15:39). Even in this moment of desolation, somehow the unifying Spirit is apparent, still glorifying the Son, still making that sonship visible, even when it looks most broken and betrayed.

In John's gospel narrative of the crucifixion, as Jesus approaches his death, he 'shares' his sonship with others. He gives his mother and his beloved disciple to each other, making the beloved disciple a 'son' like himself (John 19:26–27). This is exactly what the Holy Spirit will do for all who come into Jesus' family, the Church, where all are children of the one Father, strengthened through the Spirit, so that Christ 'may dwell in [their] hearts' (Ephesians 3:14–19).

Although it is always unwise to go beyond the careful limits of what the New Testament thinks we need to know, it is hard not to see the bond of love, the Holy Spirit, at work here in the cross. The Holy Spirit has bonded Jesus as the Son of the Father, even in his humanity, and that same embrace continues through suffering and death. The Father does not let go of the Son but continues to 'beget' him in the Spirit. The Son is 'reborn' through death because the Spirit, the Giver of Life, is not quenched by death. The cross is the most extraordinary demonstration of the binding love of God, a love so strong that nothing can make the Father cease to be the Father or the Son cease to be the Son, held in the power of the Spirit.[19]

In this unifying action of the Spirit in the life, death and resurrection of Christ, time and eternity are held together, as are life and death. God's eternal life enters into history and into death and makes itself at home there, for our sake. The unbreakable bond of love between Father, Son and Holy Spirit is stretched into time and death to make room for us, to invite us into this unity in the Spirit.

As always with the gifts of the Spirit, the gift of unifying love both comes to us from outside, from the gracious self-giving of God, and then becomes naturalised in us, enabling us to become what we are, what we were intended to be, what we long to be. The definition that John's Gospel gives of salvation is that we are given 'power to become children of God' (John 1:12), restoring in us the image in which we were created, the image of the Son of the Father in whom the Spirit lives and breathes. It is for this that the Son lives, dies and rises, held in the Father's love by the Spirit, to break into the powerful slavery and lies of sin, which work always to destroy the image of the Son in us. That power that tried and failed to break apart Father and Son on the cross tries constantly to fracture our own filial relationship with God but is defeated, over and over again, by the Spirit's powerful bond of love. The bond of love is our hope of salvation in Christ – that the Father never lets go of the Son and will not let go of us, made through the work of the Spirit into the likeness of that same Son.

Salvation, then, is not a static state of being. It has a past, present and future element to it for us. Everything necessary for our salvation has been done, once for all, upon the cross, where Christ offers for us 'a full, perfect and sufficient sacrifice, oblation and satisfaction'.[20] But daily, the Holy Spirit holds the fullness of Christ's work in the bond of love with our own reality, as we

The Holy Spirit, the Giver of Life

grow into 'the measure of the full stature of Christ' (Ephesians 4:13). Salvation remains gift, not possession, as the Holy Spirit continues to draw us into our true nature as children of God, until we come to what the Creed calls 'the life of the world to come'. Sanctification is the ongoing working of the Spirit with our spirits to grow more Christ-like, more filial, more like family to one another, more and more holy in our unity.

All of these filaments of the Spirit's unifying work are seen closely woven together in the sacraments, particularly baptism and Eucharist. Here, the history of Jesus is bound together with the eternity of the Son; God's time and our time meet, for our good. The Holy Spirit takes everyday things like water, bread and wine and binds them into the action of God, so that they can carry the story of the Son and build the life of the Son in those who participate. Every sacrament tells the story of the Son and draws those who hear and engage into their filial relationship with the Father through the Spirit.

In this, as in all things, once again, the Holy Spirit is the Jesus-maker. The Holy Spirit creates the Church to be the body of Christ. Individuals may be the temple of the Holy Spirit and the sisters and brothers of the Son, but only in union, in unity together, can they be the body of Christ. The unifying gift of the Spirit in this creation echoes the unity of God's eternal being: God is only One in Threeness and only Three in Oneness. That is the pattern of the Christian Church, too. One person is not a church, but a neither is a church one that is not full of individuals. The work of the Holy Spirit in joining us together in the body of Christ does not make us monochrome. On the contrary, as Paul says, 'There are varieties of gifts, but the same Spirit' (1 Corinthians 12:4). Our differences are part of our gift to one another. Paul goes on to point out that a body cannot function if it is all foot or all ear (1 Corinthians 12:14–31). This is an impassioned plea for a kind of unity that sees differences as necessary gifts, not as problematic, and it leads directly into Paul's description of the greatest gift of all, which is love, the Spirit's unifier.

2 The Holy Spirit as the bond of love in the theological/immanent Trinity

God, Father, Son and Holy Spirit are not in danger of fracture or division. The Holy Spirit's gift of holding unity through love is what God is, in God's very being. In human life, sanctification, the holy gift of the Holy Spirit, entails an increasing desire for God and for the flourishing of others, and this is what is discernible in the life of God. God, Father, Son and Holy Spirit love one another with such total self-giving that none can be known without the other. Their very 'names' are not about their individuality but about their relationship to one another. This is their whole definition, that each is 'named' and 'given' by the others.

Yet, at the same time, the three persons of the Trinity are not identical or interchangeable while remaining all equally God. In God's own life, there is no diminishment in dependence, no need to define one over against another. Father, Son and Holy Spirit are freely and joyfully bonded together, unwilling to be known in separation. The Father can only be known in the gift of the Son through the Spirit; the Son can only be known as the Son of the Father's self-giving in the Spirit; the Spirit can only be known in the Son's love offered back to the Father in the Spirit. Full reciprocity marks the uniting love of the Trinity. Each gives themselves in love and receives themselves back in love. That is why, in God, it is not contradictory to be at the same time One and Three – because the union is so close that those are not different states of being as they are for fragmented and self-serving human beings.

Augustine calls the Holy Spirit 'a kind of unutterable communion'.[21] And that is part of what is indicated to us by the name we use for this Third Person: Father and Son are also holy and spirit, and their relating is held in the bond of the love of the one whose name is what the others have in common. That is why it is particularly appropriate that the Spirit, the 'unutterable communion' of the Trinity, is called the bond of love, since love is the very definition of God's being.

Conclusion

The Creed's description of the Holy Spirit gives a strong base from which to explore the Third and often neglected Person of the Trinity. The Holy Spirit is the Giver of Life, God, just as the Father and the Son are – identical in their divinity but also distinguished by their relations to each other and to us. In all things, the whole being of God is involved, but that being is always Trinitarian. The Holy Spirit enables and receives worship, which brings us into the presence of God, which is what it is to glorify God. The Holy Spirit weaves the narrative of God's action with human beings and draws us into it, so it becomes our story as it is also the story of the whole world. In other words, the Holy Spirit speaks through the prophets. And the Holy Spirit nurtures and curates the community of Christ's disciples, the Church, leading them into the life of the Son for their good and for the good of all the world.

The Holy Spirit, the life-giver, is, with the Father and the Son, Creator God, breathing the life that only God can give into all living beings, and, in particular, breathing the Son-shaped life into human beings, who are called to receive and live in the gift of 'imaging' the Son's love of the Father through the life of the Spirit.

The creativity of the Holy Spirit, in union with the Father and the Son, is not limited to the Church. God is the Creator of all that is, and the Holy Spirit seeks and tends the filial response of the Son to the Father in all the ways appropriate to the diverse creation God has made. The 'image-making' aspect of the Holy Spirit's life-giving work may properly be sought for in anything that gives joy, that requires love, that seeks truth, that liberates, that enables people to receive each other as gift. The awe, wonder and sheer intellectual fascination of those who explore the universe is, in the life of the Spirit, a way of glorifying God, because it shows that creation is fatherly and filial – it is full of meaning, purpose and responsiveness. The creative arts, too, seek pattern, meaning and revelation in 'imaging', and draw people into a narrative that is not just about the lonely individual ego.[22] In creation, and particularly in the giving of the Son to humanity, God is the great image-maker and delights in a responsive image-making in creation. As created beings respond in delight and desire and longing for meaning, so they image the Son's response to the Father in the Spirit: they glorify.

The filial response to God is at the heart of the Spirit's work in all things. The Spirit always glorifies the Son and presents the Son to the Father. This is the Spirit's work of inspiration in Scripture: to bring out the way in which reality coalesces around the Son of the Father, and around the overwhelming generosity of God's self-gift in the incarnation. The Spirit glorifies the Son by making him present and living in the world that God has made, and the Spirit breathes the son- and daughter-shaped response in those who receive the Son, so that they, too, can glorify the Father.

As in all God's works towards us, Father, Son and Holy Spirit are all equally present and active in the saving work of God in Christ. The Son glorifies the Father, making God present in human life and in human death; the Son confronts the world's evil, hatred, despair, impatient selfishness and separation from God and makes this, too, a means of glorifying the Father. God is not absent in these people and places, because the Son has glorified the Father here through the life-giving Spirit. The Spirit, the bond of love, holds the relationship between the Son and the Father in reality, in the life, death, resurrection and ascension of the Son. Nothing can break apart the love of God. Salvation is God's ever-faithful offer of relationship, endlessly recreating the Father's love of the Son in the Spirit as invitation. All are invited to become children of God, as the Son glorifies the Father in all things, and the Spirit breathes the Son's loving response to the Father, 'Abba, Father', in a fresh act of creation 'in the image'.

In all this, two defining concepts in relation to the work of the Holy Spirit stand out.

1 The Jesus-maker

In the Spirit's work in the world, the Spirit is always the Jesus-maker. All the Spirit's gifts are to enable the fuller glory, the fuller revelation of the heartbeat of all that is, which is the Father's love of the Son and the Son's love of the Father. The name of that love is Holy Spirit. The Holy Spirit constantly gives life to the longing and gives the capacity, the power and the freedom to become children of God in the image of the Son. There is a self-effacing power at work in the Spirit, who does not desire to be at the centre but always glorifies the Son. But that self-effacing dynamic is at work in all the ways in which we encounter God. The Father is only known in the Son and the Son is only known through the Spirit; the Spirit is known as the Son-maker, and the Father is known as the giver of the Son-shaped Spirit. The circling dance of mutual love and glorification can be entered at any point and always leads to the fullness of God's self-gift in creation.

This Jesus-making aspect of the work of the Spirit is at the heart of the life of the Church. This is what the Church is for: to help to realise the Christ-shaped response of the world to God. In worship, in sacraments, in prayer, in preaching and in searching the Scriptures, in life together, in witness, in acknowledging failure and in seeking and offering forgiveness, in all the manifold activities of the Church, the Spirit is at work to build the body of Christ to the glory of God. In each individual and in the new community of faith, inexorably, the Spirit teaches us the Son's prayer to the Father: 'Abba'. Even in our passionate disagreements, the Spirit is not absent. There are varieties of gifts but the same Spirit. If disagreement is offered as gift to the body of Christ – calling it to truth and unity, longing for its greater flourishing and its deepening response to God – it is nothing to fear. But expect that disagreements among those whom the Spirit is making into children of God will come to the time of testing, when the Spirit will lead us to the moment in the garden of Gethsemane. 'Not my will but yours' (Luke 22:42) is the response the Spirit grows in the Church, the body of Christ. When disagreement becomes self-will and self-definition rather than seeking together to grow our likeness of Christ, then the Spirit is grieved. Then it is time to 'Put away from you all bitterness and wrath and anger and wrangling and slander, together with all malice, and be kind to one another, tender-hearted, forgiving one another, as God in Christ has forgiven you' (Ephesians 4:31–32).

2 The hinge between time and eternity

The Jesus-making work of the Spirit ties in closely with the other defining concept in relation to the work of the Spirit, which is that the Spirit is the hinge between time and eternity, between the life of Christ lived in history and the eternal relationship between the Father and the Son in the love of the Spirit. The Spirit explains the world, not just in words but in lives lived as children of God. The Spirit is, from creation through to the life of the world to come, the interpreter of God, connecting God's transcendent life with God's life of self-giving to the world.

That is why it is the work of the Spirit that enables us to say, 'We believe.' The Creed starts with creation and ends with the life of the world to come, and in all of this, God, Father, Son and Holy Spirit are present and active. The Holy Spirit's work of building the body of Christ gives us the liberty and the trust to see the world for what it is and to continue to work and pray, in faith, for the coming of the kingdom. As we say, 'We believe,' we are exercising our filial capacity. Just as Jesus, through the power of the Spirit, responded in all things good and bad as the Son of the Father, so we, too, believe that this divine self-giving love is at work to shape us and our world and to invite it home.

To say that 'we believe' is an act of trust, but it is not a blind one. The more the Spirit draws us into our reality as children of God, the more the world makes sense, the more 'we believe'. Like Jesus, the Son incarnate through the power of the Spirit, we trust in the fatherliness of God, and as we live in trust and hope, the Spirit builds in and through us the image of the Son, to glorify, to make visible and effective, the love of God, Father, Son and Holy Spirit.

Questions for further thought

1 Why do you think the connection between the evangelical and the theological Trinity is important for us in our daily lives?
2 Do you recognise Paul's description of our lack of freedom to choose what we long to be?

3 Is it a good image of our discipleship to think of ourselves as growing more and more like the Son through the Spirit? The word used here is 'filial' – daughters and sons.
4 Does it illuminate your understanding of the Holy Spirit to say that Holy Spirit is the name of God's love?

Notes

Introduction
1 Augustine of Hippo, Letter 25.3; Julian of Norwich, *Revelations of Divine Love* 59; and see, for example, Bernard of Clairvaux, *Sermon on the Song of Songs*.

I A creedal world
1 This is how the final paragraph of the Creed usually appears, though there is sometimes a break between the affirmation of the Spirit and the affirmation of the Church:

> We believe in the Holy Spirit,
>> the Lord, the giver of life,
>> who proceeds from the Father and the Son,
>> who with the Father and the Son is worshipped and glorified,
>> who has spoken through the prophets.
>> We believe in one holy catholic and apostolic Church.
>> We acknowledge one baptism for the forgiveness of sins.
>> We look for the resurrection of the dead,
>> and the life of the world to come.

2 This is a prayer over the water of baptism in the Church of England *Common Worship* baptism service:

> We thank you, almighty God, for the gift of water

to sustain, refresh and cleanse all life.
Over water the Holy Spirit moved in the beginning
   of creation.
Through water you led the children of Israel
from slavery in Egypt to freedom in the Promised
   Land.
In water your Son Jesus received the baptism of John
and was anointed by the Holy Spirit as the Messiah,
   the Christ,
to lead us from the death of sin to newness of life.

See *Common Worship: Services and Prayers of the Church of England*, 'Prayer over the Water' (London: Church House Publishing, 2024), p. 355.

3 I have written about these two related functions of creeds, as pathways and boundaries, in Nathan Eddy and Graham Tomlin (eds), *The Bond of Peace* (London: SPCK, 2021).
4 There has already been a great deal of excellent writing on the Creed. See, for example, Alex Irving, *We Believe: Exploring the Nicene Faith* (Nottingham: Apollos, 2022).
5 A formidable, painstaking and scholarly tracing of the historical and geographical evolution of creeds is to be found in Wolfram Kinzig, *A History of Early Christian Creeds* (Berlin: de Gruyter, 2024).
6 The movement was variously called 'Macedonians', 'Tropici' or 'Pneumatomachians'. We have almost no extant writings from their point of view, only from those who opposed them, like Basil the Great and Gregory of Nyssa, who wrote *On the Holy Spirit, Against the Macedonians*.
7 'In consequence, in their glory He has no share, to equal honour with them He has no claim; and that, as for power, He possesses only so much of it as is sufficient for the partial activities assigned to Him; that with the creative force He is

quite disconnected.' Gregory of Nyssa, *On the Holy Spirit, Against the Macedonians.*

2 The case for the Holy Spirit: the Cappadocian Fathers

1. These methods are usually called 'Scripture, tradition, reason and experience'. Although 'experience' was not part of the original 'three-legged stool', that was partly because our understanding of what constitutes 'experience' and 'reason' has changed. Before the Enlightenment, they would have been seen as much more interconnected.
2. There are a number of Christian churches that accepted the Nicene Creed but not its later clarification in the fifth century, and a Western addition to the Creed concerning the relationship between the Holy Spirit and the other two persons of the Trinity was part of the cause of a major schism between Eastern Orthodox and Western churches, so this statement of unity is very much a generalisation.
3. For a good general introduction to the theology and work of the Cappadocian Fathers, see Anthony Meredith, *The Cappadocians* (Chicago: Geoffrey Chapman, 1995).
4. See Gregory of Nyssa, 'Fourth Homily on Ecclesiastes', in Stuart G. Hall (ed.), *Gregory of Nyssa, Homilies on Ecclesiastes* (Berlin: de Gruyter, 1993).
5. To read Gregory of Nyssa's orations, see 'Select Orations', New Advent: https://www.newadvent.org/fathers/3102.htm (accessed 13 February 2025).
6. Gregory of Nyssa, *On the Holy Spirit, Against the Macedonians:* 'These clever people must tell us how one perfect thing can be more perfect or less perfect than another perfect thing; for so long as the definition of perfection applies to it, that thing can not admit of a greater and a less in the matter of perfection.'
7. Basil the Great, *On the Holy Spirit* 18.47

8 Gregory of Nyssa, *On the Holy Spirit, Against the Macedonians*.
9 Gregory of Nazianzus, *Fifth Theological Oration* XXIX.
10 Gregory of Nyssa, *On the Holy Spirit, Against the Macedonians*.
11 Basil the Great, *On the Holy Spirit* 9.
12 Basil the Great, *On the Holy Spirit* 16.39.
13 Gregory of Nazianzus, *Fifth Theological Oration* XII.
14 C. S. Lewis, *Mere Christianity* (London: William Collins, 2012).
15 Gregory of Nazianzus, *Third Theological Oration* III.
16 Gregory of Nazianzus, *Fifth Theological Oration* IX: 'But the difference of manifestation, if I may so express myself, or rather of their mutual relations one to another, has caused the difference of their Names.'
17 Cf. Frances Young's lecture at St Mellitus College as part of the Nicaea Project, in which she picks up the point about the names. God's self-naming in Jesus, the Son, is equally about God's commitment to us. See 'Revd. Professor Frances Young: "A Question of Identity: Creature or Creator"', St Mellitus College McDonald Agape Nicea Project: https://stmellitus.ac.uk/nicaea (accessed 13 February 2025).
18 Basil the Great, *On the Holy Spirit* 17.43: 'What thing ever lost its own nature by being numbered? Is it not the fact that things when numbered remain what they naturally and originally were?'
19 The Cappadocian Fathers were Greek-speaking: they use the technical language of one *Ousia* and three *hypostases*; the Latin-speaking debate uses the language of 'essence' or 'substance' for the Unity and 'persona' for the Trinity.

3 The case for the Holy Spirit: Augustine of Hippo

1. There is so much written about Augustine that it is hard to know where to start. His own journey of self-discovery in God is described in *Confessions,* translated many times. See, for example, Henry Chadwick (London: Oxford University Press, 1998); Sarah Ruden (London: Penguin Modern Library, 2018). Good introductions to Augustine include Cally Hammond, *Augustine's Life of Prayer, Learning and Love* (Abingdon: Bible Reading Fellowship, 2019); James K. A. Smith, *On the Road with St Augustine* (Grand Rapids: Brazos, 2019).
2. Augustine, *De Trinitate* 2.4.
3. Augustine, *De Trinitate* 4.21.30.
4. Augustine, *De Trinitate* 4.21.20.
5. T. J. White describes this as showing how we might understand 'immaterial processions'. See T. J. White, *The Trinity* (Washington, DC: Catholic University of America Press, 2022), p. 112.
6. Augustine, *De Trinitate* 8.10.14.
7. Augustine, *De Trinitate* 14.8.11: 'For although the human mind is not of the same nature with God, yet the image of that nature than which none is better, is to be sought and found in us.'
8. Augustine, *De Trinitate* 14.14.18.
9. Augustine, *De Trinitate* 9.9.14.
10. Augustine, *De Trinitate* 14.13.17.
11. Augustine, *De Trinitate* 7.6.11.
12. Augustine, *De Trinitate* 5.16.17: 'Therefore that which begins to be spoken of God in time, and which was not spoken of Him before, is manifestly spoken of Him relatively,' that is, in relation to us but not in a way that changes God.
13. Cf. Mark 1:11 and the parallel accounts of Jesus' baptism for the voice of the Father and the descent of the Spirit as a

dove; cf. Acts 2:1–4 for the Holy Spirit as tongues of flame; Augustine, *De Trinitate* 2.6.11.

4 The Holy Spirit defended: summarising the arguments

1. Augustine suggests that the simplest way for us to grasp this is to say that all the persons send themselves and each other. As with all acts of God towards us, the whole of God is involved. Augustine, *De Trinitate* 2.5.9.
2. Augustine, *De Trinitate* 7.4.7–8.

5 The Holy Spirit in the Creed

1. See Wolfram Kinzig, *A History of Early Christian Creeds* (Berlin: de Gruyter, 2024).
2. 'New English Translation of the Divine Liturgy', Melkite Catholic Eparty of Newton: https://melkite.org/faith/faith-worship/new-english-translation-of-the-divine-liturgy (accessed 13 February 2025).
3. Basil the Great, *On the Holy Spirit* 16.38.
4. This is, obviously, a distinctively Christian reading of Genesis. It must always be remembered that the first home of what we call the Old Testament is with the Jewish people, who do not read this passage as Trinitarian.
5. The word 'monarchia' does not mean 'monarchy' but 'origin' or 'source'.
6. This practice seems to have started from the sixth century in the Latin-speaking part of the Christian world and was officially endorsed by the Pope in the eleventh century.
7. The earlier form of the Creed, before the addition of the filioque clause, said that the Holy Spirit 'proceeds from the Father. With the Father and the Son, he is worshipped and glorified.'
8. Cf. John 12:27–28. David Ford's commentary on John's Gospel is particularly helpful in bringing out the theme of

'glory' in the gospel. See David Ford, *The Gospel of John: A Theological Commentary* (Grand Rapids: Baker Academic, 2022).

9 See Donald Berry, *Glory in Romans and the Unified Purpose of God in Redemptive History* (Eugene, OR: Wipf & Stock, 2016).

10 Cf. Isaiah; Jeremiah 1:4–19; Ezekiel 1–5.

11 It is always hard to tell exactly what ancient 'heretics' believed, since they are generally described by their opponents rather than in their own words. We do know that the great North African theologian Tertullian was associated with Montanism in the second century, and that in many parts of the Christian world, there seemed little difference between Montanists and 'orthodox' Christians. Some have argued that the fledgling church was suspicious of Montanists because of the leadership roles permitted to women prophets. See, for example, Christine Trevett, *Montanism: Gender, Authority and the New Prophecy* (Cambridge: Cambridge University Press, 1996).

12 See Kinzig, *A History of Early Christian Creeds*, pp. 172–5.

13 *Common Worship*, The Declaration of Assent: https://www.churchofengland.org/prayer-and-worship/worship-texts-and-resources/common-worship/ministry/declaration-assent (accessed 13 February 2025).

14 An opening collect for the baptism service reads:

> Heavenly Father,
>   by the power of your Holy Spirit
>   you give to your faithful people new life in the
>   water of baptism.
>   Guide and strengthen us by the same Spirit,
>   that we who are born again may serve you in faith
>   and love,

and grow into the full stature of your Son, Jesus
  Christ,
who is alive and reigns with you in the unity of
  the Holy Spirit
now and for ever.
Common Worship, 'The Collect', p. 350.

15 See N. T. Wright, *The Resurrection of the Son of God* (London: SPCK, 2017).

6 The Holy Spirit, the Giver of Life

1 Catherine Mowry LaCugna, *God with Us: The Trinity and Christian Life* (New York: Harper Collins, 1991), p. 1.
2 Jürgen Moltmann was an unashamed 'social Trinitarian', arguing that the emphasis on the divine unity in Western theology had prevented a fully Trinitarian understanding, such as the Creed requires. Moltmann suggests that we should think of the Trinity as a 'family'. See Jürgen Moltmann, *The Trinity and the Kingdom of God* (New York: Harper & Row, 1981), p. 199.
3 T. F. Torrance, *The Christian Doctrine of God: One Being, Three Persons* (Edinburgh: T&T Clark, 1996), p. 7
4 Anthony Thiselton speaks of a 'narrative approach' to the doctrine of the Trinity – simply following through the New Testament account and noticing the intrinsic assumptions about the presence of Father, Son and Holy Spirit. See Anthony Thiselton, *A Shorter Guide to the Holy Spirit: Bible, Doctrine, Experience* (Grand Rapids: Eerdmans, 2015), p. 71.
5 Medieval painters sometimes depict Mary as receiving the Holy Spirit's 'overshadowing' in the form of a dove whispering in her ear, signifying her receptiveness and that this is an act of her will and mind.

6 Thiselton describes the Holy Spirit as Agent in Jesus' baptism, cf. Thiselton, *A Shorter Guide to the Holy Spirit*, p. 23.
7 Paul picks up and expands on this double symbolism of baptism as life and death (cf. Romans 6:3–4).
8 For a fuller list and discussion of references to the Holy Spirit in the work of Jesus, see Veli-Matti Kärkkäinen, *Pneumatology: The Holy Spirit in Ecumenical, International and Contextual Perspective* (Grand Rapids: Baker Books, 2018), pp. 15–22.
9 The idea of 'reading back' from the economic Trinitarian action of God into the immanent reality of God is not new; it is how Trinitarian theology is possible at all. But many of the ideas in this section were sparked by Thomas Weinandy, *The Father's Spirit of Sonship: Reconceiving the Trinity* (Edinburgh: T&T Clark, 1995).
10 This is sometimes labelled patripassianism, meaning that the Father also suffers.
11 The best example of this theology is in the work of Jürgen Moltmann. See, for example, Jürgen Moltmann, *The Crucified God* (London: SCM, 1974).
12 For a fuller discussion of what is at stake here, see Thomas Weinandy, 'Does God Suffer?', First Things: https://www.firstthings.com/article/2001/11/does-god-suffer (accessed 13 February 2025); Thomas Weinandy, *Does God Suffer?* (Notre Dame: University of Notre Dame Press, 2020).
13 It is important to bear in mind that these are Jewish Scriptures, differently read by Jewish believers, who do not find Trinitarian references here, though as Christians, we are bound to.
14 Athanasius, *On the Incarnation of the Word* 14.
15 For the best creative theological engagement with Athanasius's theology, see Khaled Anatolios, *Deification Through the Cross: An Eastern Christian Theology of*

Salvation (Grand Rapids: Eerdmans, 2020).

16 Thomas Weinandy puts it like this: the Holy Spirit is 'the one in whom the Father begets the Son, conforms the Father to be Father for the Son and conforms the Son to be the Son for the Father'. Thomas Weinandy, *The Father's Spirit of Sonship* (Edinburgh: T&T Clark, 1995), p. 17.

17 John's Gospel does not record Jesus' cry from the cross, 'My God, my God, why have you forsaken me?' which is the opening verse of Psalm 22. This deliberate reference to Psalm 22 earlier in the crucifixion narrative suggests that John knew of Jesus' cry and deliberately echoes the echoes.

18 Sarah Coakley puts forward a strong Trinitarian theology of prayer. See Sarah Coakley, *God, Sexuality and the Self* (Cambridge: Cambridge University Press, 2014), p. 111.

19 See Eberhard Jüngel, *God as the Mystery of the World* (Grand Rapids: Eerdmans, 1983); John Webster, *Eberhard Jüngel: An Introduction to His Theology* (Cambridge: Cambridge University Press, 1986). Jüngel's account of a Trinitarian theology of the cross is more nuanced than Moltmann's, which we have discussed above.

20 *Common Worship*, 'Eucharistic Prayer C', p. 192.

21 Augustine, *De Trinitate* 5.11.12.

22 For a fuller exploration of the Holy Spirit at work in creativity, see John McIntyre, *The Shape of Pneumatology: Studies in the Doctrine of the Holy Spirit* (Edinburgh: T&T Clark, 1997).

Suggested further reading

Anatolios, Khaled, *Retrieving Nicaea: The Development and Meaning of Trinitarian Doctrine* (Grand Rapids: Baker Academic, 2018).
Bird, Michael, *What Christians Ought to Believe* (Grand Rapids: Zondervan, 2016).
Chadwick, Henry, *Augustine of Hippo: A Life* (Oxford: Oxford University Press, 2010).
Coakley, Sarah, *God, Sexuality and the Self: An Essay 'On the Trinity'* (Cambridge: Cambridge University Press, 2013).
Collins, Paul, *The Trinity: A Guide for the Perplexed* (Edinburgh: T&T Clark, 2008).
Irving, Alex, *We Believe: Exploring the Nicene Faith* (London: IVP, 2021).
Kinzig, Wolfram, *A History of Early Christian Creeds* (Berlin: de Gruyter, 2024).
Leyden, Michael, *Faithful Living: Discipleship, Creed and Ethics* (London: SCM, 2019).
Meredith, Anthony, *The Cappadocians* (New York: St Vladimir's Seminary Press, 2004).
Smail, Thomas, *The Giving Gift: The Holy Spirit in Person* (London: Darton, Longman & Todd, 1994).
Smith, James K. A., *On the Road with St Augustine* (Grand Rapids: Brazos, 2019).
Tanner, Kathryn, *Jesus, Humanity and the Trinity* (Edinburgh: T&T Clark, 2001).
Tomlin, Graham, *The Prodigal Spirit* (London: Alpha International, 2011).

Suggested further reading

Weinandy, Thomas, *The Father's Spirit of Sonship* (Eugene, OR: Wipf & Stock, 2011).

White, T. J., *The Trinity: On the Nature and Mystery of the One God* (Washington, DC: Catholic University of America, 2022).

Whitworth, Patrick, *Three Wise Men from the East: The Cappadocian Fathers and the Struggle for Orthodoxy* (Durham: Sacristy Press, 2015).

Yong, Amos, *Spirit, Word, Community: Theological Hermeneutics in Trinitarian Perspective* (Eugene, OR: Wipf & Stock, 2006).

Young, Frances, *The Making of the Creeds* (London: SCM, 2002).

www.ingramcontent.com/pod-product-compliance
Lightning Source LLC
Chambersburg PA
CBHW050528170426
43201CB00013B/2123